AWESOME RECIPES & KITCHEN SHORTCUTS

SAM THE COOKING GUY

AWESOME RECIPES & KITCHEN SHORTCUTS

SAM ZIEN

WILEY

JOHN WILEY & SONS, INC.

Copyright © 2010 by Sam Zien. All rights reserved
Photography by Steve Sanders and Josh Henry

Published by John Wiley & Sons, Inc., Hoboken, New Jersey
Published simultaneously in Canada

For general information on our other products and services or for technical support, please contact our Customer Care Department within the United States at (800) 762-2974, outside the United States at (317) 572-3993 or fax (317) 572-4002.

Wiley also publishes its books in a variety of electronic formats. Some content that appears in print may not be available in electronic books. For more information about Wiley products, visit our Web site at www.wiley.com.

Design by Joline Rivera

Library of Congress Cataloging-in-Publication Data
Zien, Sam.
    Sam the cooking guy: awesome recipes and kitchen shortcuts / Sam
Zien.
        p. cm.
    Includes index.
    ISBN 978-0-470-46794-7 (pbk.)
 1. Quick and easy cookery. 1. Title.
    TX833.5.Z524 2010
    641.5'55--dc22

Printed in the United States of America
10 9 8 7 6 5 4 3 2 1

To all those who did something when everyone said you couldn't.
Way to fricking go.

contents

ACKNOWLEDGMENTS

First, and foremost, thank you to anyone who bought the first book, because you made this one possible. Without you, there's none of this and for that I am hugely grateful. And for those who didn't buy the first book—really?

My family—Kelly, May, Jordan, and Zack. I love you all the days.

To Justin—For your support and guarded council, again. And I hope I can continue to do things that make you say, "Wow, I really didn't expect that!"

To Gypsy—you were a big part of the success of book one, thank you. But stop reading this now and go promote it.

To the Lashers—For everything, but especially your patience. You both are such a huge part of this.

Erin—For your testing and tasting. You're my favorite Ginger, ever.

Jana—For your help turning my nonsense into organization.

Amy Laskin—For well . . . you know.

Steve, I mean Gary. Hopefully you can shoot all my stuff—you're a great talent and a great friend.

And my brother, Richard—You didn't actually help with anything, but you still haven't gotten over my choice of Randy as best man—and I feel bad. Hope this makes up for it.

INTRODUCTION

I had an epiphany one day while working on this book. My last book, *Just a Bunch of Recipes*, was based on simple stuff: simple ingredients, simple steps, simple whatever—that was it. So if this book was going to be about shortcuts, it needed to be even more simple, right? Right. So one evening I share this idea with my wife, Kelly, and she totally disagrees. "If you do that," she said, "it'll just be a bunch of recipes using a can of mushroom soup, and that'll be gross." Wow, can't you just feel her anger? Why you hatin' on the mushroom soup, Kelly? So of course I do the same thing I always do when we have a moment like this: I put my hands over my ears and scream, "I can't hear you, I can't hear you!!"

But I've pretty much made a career out of showing people they can eat well without it taking forever—hassle-free, simple recipes with only a few ingredients. And the simpler the better, it seems, because no matter where I go, people always mention the easy shortcuts that have really changed the way they cook (and eat). That's why I love the idea of this book. Whether it's using a deli-roasted chicken for a fake pulled pork sandwich (page 123), combining previously frozen pasta with sour cream and chili sauce for a really quick dinner (page 176) or busting out a tub of premade pesto for about a jillion things—hopefully it'll get people cooking.

It turns out, the hardest part was deciding how to organize the recipes, because many of them fit in multiple chapters. I wanted just one giant chapter simply titled Totally Great & Easy Frickin' Stuff, but some people (no names here, Kelly), didn't think that was a good idea.

So this will be part cookbook and a lot guidebook. There will be recipes, there will be shortcuts, and there will also be plenty of advice. And the advice might just be a suggestion or two at times, but I really hope you listen, because I want you to be a participant in your own food life, not just a bystander. It's the classic "give a man a fish and he eats for a day. Teach a man to fish and he eats forever." Hopefully, we're learning to fish here.

—Sam the Cooking Guy, March 2010

(Oh, and I've added two canned mushroom soup recipes, just for Kelly. Check out pages 209 and 220.)

"I WANT YOU TO BE A PARTICIPANT IN YOUR OWN FOOD LIFE, NOT JUST A BY-STANDER."

This is not a completely normal cookbook, and there are definitely a few things you should know before getting started. Here they are:

GROUND RULES FOR USING THIS BOOK

1. This book is about using what you have. And, of course, you can't make a recipe unless you have the ingredients, but that's not what I mean. I mean using the things that you'd normally have in your cupboard, pantry, fridge or wherever to make great-tasting and easy junk (see #2). At no point should you ever look at a recipe and wonder what something is and where the hell you'd get it. I'll leave craziness like that to the other cookbook people.

2. When I say junk, I don't really mean "junk." I mean "stuff."

3. Not everything in this book will be in a traditional "recipe" format. A lot of it will be in a nontraditional "suggestion" format. So if you see something that looks like advice rather than a recipe, take the advice and do whatever it says.

4. Before you cook anything, read the recipe all the way through first. And that advice goes for this book or anyone else's (especially anyone else's). You just never know what will pop up in the instructions that you aren't prepared for. Oh, sure, you might have all the ingredients, but then you get to a line that says:

"Pour everything into a 19th-century clay baguette pan that's been rubbed with succotash oil and stored in an underground cellar at 47°F for 3 weeks."

You think I'm kidding? Ever watched the Food Network?

5. Don't freak about not having an ingredient. Recipes should be viewed as a guide, that's it. Substitute, change, switch, add more, add less—just do whatever the hell you need to do to make it. Just because I say onion rings on the Pulled Chicken Sandwich are amazing (and they are), if you hate onions, swap them for something else. Cookbooks should be as much about inspiration as they are about recipes. Make them your own.

6. Okay, this one's really important: When a recipe says oil, unless I specify exactly what type of oil, I don't care what you use. I'm not being mean here, I'm just saying that pretty much whatever you pick will work. That is assuming your selection is not a flavored one like garlic oil, sesame oil, thyme oil, etc. Everything else—vegetable, canola, peanut, regular olive oil—will be fine. My goal is to get you more comfortable in the kitchen, and that comes from you having the freedom to

do what you want and not feel handcuffed. Hey, I realize this pretty much goes against every cookbook ever written, and I don't care.

Quality ingredients are always important, and using good stuff is the way to go. But (and this is the part that will forever prevent me from winning a James Beard Foundation cookbook award), there's a time for all things. I only mean that if you're serving a simple piece of seared tuna with pretty much nothing else, you should buy a good piece of tuna. But let's say instead you're making the Cap'n Crunch® Seared Tuna on page 71 (which, in addition to having been coated with a children's cereal, is also accompanied by a mix of mayo, mustard, and hot Asian chili sauce). Spending $100 on a pound of tuna would be moronic. In this case, you can certainly use the fresh tuna your everyday supermarket has. In fact I keep blocks of tuna in my freezer specifically for this recipe and it always comes out fantastic. Look, I can't say this strongly enough: Don't not make something because you think you need to spend a ton on it. I'd rather you make your own version of it than not make it at all.

That's it.

Open it, scope it, and cook something.

> "HEY, I REALIZE THIS PRETTY MUCH GOES AGAINST EVERY COOKBOOK EVER WRITTEN, AND I DON'T CARE."

I thought it would be useful to give you an idea of how I use some of the items in my pantry. Not just a listing, but a brief description of how I use them—because all this stuff will show up in the book.

THE SHORTCUT PANTRY

OIL

After my opening remarks about oil (page 14), I should clarify a bit. Oil is oil. Get it? It pretty much does one thing—it lubricates.

These basic oils:
vegetable
canola
peanut
regular olive oil (not extra virgin)

are fine to use wherever you want because they don't give off too much flavor, and for most things you don't want flavor, you just want the lubrication (okay, I've gotta stop saying that.) And just so you know, peanut oil tends to smoke at a higher temperature than others, so it's ideal for cooking over really high heat, like in a wok. But unless someone at the table has a peanut allergy, feel free to use whatever oil you want.

And now for the good stuff . . . extra virgin olive oil is what you get after you press olives for the first time. It's normally way bolder and fruitier than regular olive oil, and every so often I'll specify it in a recipe because I want to add some big-ass flavor to the dish. It's also a lot like cowboy boots in that it's a personal preference—not every pair fits every foot, so to speak. And this is why cookware stores let you sample it with dipping bread before you buy. Use it when I say so, and even though it's been reduced to a completely overused and misused acronym (EVOO), resist the urge to do everything with it, including washing your pets.

PASTA—DRIED, FRESH, OR FROZEN

Such an important topic, I wrote a whole chapter on it—see page 167.

DELI-ROASTED CHICKEN

So great, it also gets its own chapter—see page 117.

CHICKEN STOCK OR BROTH

You don't need to be Martha Stewart to keep this on hand. The terms "stock" and "broth" are quite interchangeable and you can find really good ones these days in those large juice-box kinda containers. You'll use it in a lot of things, including the ridiculously easy Pea Soup on page 219—one of my all-time favorites. If you just put some plain broth in a pot over low heat and started adding almost anything out of your fridge—veggies, meats, shrimp— in about an hour you'd have a pretty amazing soup. Try it sometime. It's a cool thing to do.

CANNED TOMATOES

This is another thing that's easy to keep in the pantry but also easy to forget you have. Add some, squishing them as you go, to cooked ground beef in a pan and you're 95 percent of the way toward a simple meat sauce.

Canned tomatoes heated with some cream cheese or mascarpone in a pot and then tossed with just-cooked pasta makes a quick little treat.

- HORSERADISH
- SHU DIXON
- GOLDEN CURRY
- SOUR DOUGH.
- TOMOLIVES
- SOFT SOAP.
- STAR MIX

ROASTED RED PEPPERS

These are so big in my house it's crazy. In a jar with or without oil, with or without garlic—it doesn't matter. They just go in so many things, they're a must-have.

They make the most versatile sauce ever (page 42), can become part of a baguette thing for an appetizer (page 68), or can even be stuffed into a split chicken breast. And I didn't even mention their transformational properties when simply added to a turkey sandwich or a pizza.

FROZEN STEAKS

Don't even . . . I get grief all the time about this idea until I cook for someone and then it's okay. You can buy thinner cuts of meat—like a "flatiron" or a "skirt steak"—that are frozen in those bags with the air sucked out, and they unfreeze quickly and easily (yes, & I know "unfreeze" is probably not so good English). I take one out, put it in its little bag in cold water, and in about 30-ish minutes it'll be ready to grill, panfry, broil, stir-fry, or whatever. My friend Joe only gets steaks from a place in Chicago and they come frozen and are some of the best steaks I've ever had. Of course, you can make it to the store and back in that time—but I'm just saying, this is way easy. And this is about easy, right? Don't overlook this idea.

ALREADY COOKED BACON, AKA "READY" BACON

If you're not into this yet, you need to be. Adding a little of this kind of bacon can really change the whole flavor of something. And the fact that it is freakishly shelf-stable until you open it means you can always have some around. Need a little encouragement? Check out the Blue Cheese Gnocchi with Bacon on page 178, the Blue Cheese Bacon–Stuffed Dates on page 67, or the Bacon Guacamole (yes, I said that) on page 60.

SPICES

I always get asked about which spices I use most often, so here's my lineup:

Cumin—for anything Mexican tasting

Curry—for anything curry tasting

Cayenne—for a little heat

Rosemary—on lamb, potatoes, beef, mushrooms

Red pepper flakes—anything with tomatoes

Dill—maybe just because I'm Jewish

Kosher salt—of course and not just because of the Jewish thing

Freshly ground pepper—absolutely

Don't get sucked into buying a million spices—they'll just go bad. And those prepackaged variety packs are a waste. They always have weird crap you'll never use. If you're not sure, go to a store that sells in bulk and just buy a little of what you need.

WHIPPING CREAM (AKA HEAVY CREAM)

Might seem a little dopey, but it comes in handy—and not just for whipping cream, ya know? Use it for absolutely last-minute pasta sauces, for soups, for sides (Creamed Spinach with Bacon, page 222), and even for desserts (Chocolate & Grand Marnier Fondue, page 249). And if it wasn't obvious, this is a terrible thing to keep in your pantry—use your fridge.

OFF-THE-SHELF SAUCES YOU REALLY SHOULD HAVE

I often get crap from people who say I'm too much into the Asian food world. But these are the same people who love what I make. And they love what I make because it doesn't taste like what everyone else makes, so forget about them. Just do what I tell you, and you'll be fine.

Jarred Pasta Sauce

Clearly not just for pasta. It has a lot of uses, but don't get too fancy buying it. Just keep a few plain jars of it around and:

• Spread a little on grilled or broiled bread with a sprinkle of Parmesan as an appetizer.

• Spread some underneath a piece of seared fish with nothing more than a drizzle of extra virgin olive oil—not only will it be good, but it'll look amazing.

• Spread on a pizza crust, but you knew that, right?

• Add as a sauce on the inside of a sandwich—I'm thinking a toasted meatloaf sandwich would be good here.

• And, of course, even on pasta . . . but make it a little pink and a little more delicate by simmering it with a little whipping cream (see page 173).

my sauces

Hoisin Sauce

This is essentially a Chinese barbeque-like sauce. You can get it at any supermarket and just having it will make your food better. Mix some with a little soy for dipping or stir-frying. Or on the oh-so-good Spicy Chinese Chicken Pizza on page 126.

Asian Chili Sauce

This is often referred to as "rooster sauce" because the most well-known brand (Sriracha®) has a rooster on the bottle. You'll be blown away by how just a little bit can impact everything from a hot dog to soups, noodles, sauces, pastas, etc. Give the Thai Curry Noodle Soup a whirl (page 111).

Not-Asian Chili Sauce

You can use this anywhere you'd use ketchup—it just has more flavor. In fact, if you had to choose between ketchup or this chili sauce, I'd buy the chili sauce because it's just better. On a sandwich, in a meatloaf, in some pasta—everywhere.

Worcestershire Sauce

A good splash of this in any soup, sauce, Bloody Mary, stew, or almost anything is good. I mean really good. Remember, this is about something small that can make a big change—Worcestershire sauce does exactly that. And while I'm on the subject . . .

Jarred Gravy

Who makes their own gravy anymore? I certainly don't. In fact, I always have a bunch of jars in my pantry for whatever might pop up. I keep both chicken and beef, whether it's beef gravy in Meatball Stroganoff (page 212) or chicken gravy in Poutine (page 203), it's all so good.

The crazy thing about gravy is that it really can go with pretty much everything. I mean, if it goes with a shrimp and egg thing, imagine what it can do to leftover and dried-out chicken, pork, or beef? (And by the way, the shrimp and egg thing is on page 195.)

Packaged Hollandaise Sauce

Scratch Hollandaise can be a huge pain, so keeping a pack or two of this in the cupboard will make life much easier. A little on asparagus or broccoli is simple genius. And of course the addition of some to the king of all breakfast dishes, the "Benedict," will transform your weekend. Just decide what the Benny will be, and you're set. See the Breakfast section (page 73) for more.

Basic BBQ Sauce

Using a tiny bit of BBQ sauce here or there can change so many things. Mixing it with a bit of mayo for a sandwich, with some chipotle sauce on a steak or with chicken, turned into the BBQ Cole Slaw on page 107 or in the Pulled Chicken Sandwich on page 123 will make everyone happy.

"...THEY **LOVE** WHAT I MAKE BECAUSE IT DOESN'T TASTE LIKE WHAT EVERYONE ELSE MAKES ..."

BTW

BTW, BBQ sauces aren't only used when you're barbequing. They're for sandwiches—like on meatloaf, or putting on a pizza or whatever. But when you do grill with a BBQ sauce, be careful.

BBQ Sauce Warning: Because of the sweet nature of most BBQ sauces, you MUST resist the urge to add the sauce at the beginning of the grilling process. If you do, the sugars will burn whatever it is you're cooking, which is fine if you're going for some nasty-tasting thing. But if you're not, start basting only in the last 5 minutes or so of cooking—and then again always just before you serve.

On the back of my very first sam the cooking guy T-shirt was written:

"WHOEVER SAID YOU EAT WITH YOUR EYES IS AN IDIOT. I EAT WITH MY MOUTH."

Of course I thought I was being funny, but the thing is, you see whatever's on the plate before you get to taste it, and if it looks like crap, it really doesn't matter how it tastes. Most things you put on a plate will look way better with a little something on top. So here are a few "looking-good-on-the-plate" rules.

SAUCES, ETC.

- garnish, garnish, garnish

- if you plate it, they will eat it . . . all of it

- asian bbq sauce - spicy bbq sauce

- pesto - pesto garlic bread

- salsa cream - honey-mustard sauce

- roasted red pepper sauce

- sweet chili soy sauce

- horseradish, the sauce

- wasabi mayo

- chipotle mayo

GARNISH, GARNISH, GARNISH

It doesn't matter what's on the plate, it can almost always use something extra. Here are the easiest garnishes to use:

- Something green like a little chopped cilantro or parsley. If you only had this stuff, you could take care of about 95 percent of your garnishing needs. Of course it would get boring after a while, but you could do it.

- Freshly ground black pepper—sounds dull? Imagine a plate of fettuccine Alfredo. It's all beige. Now give it a few grinds of black pepper and voilà: dull no more.

- A few chopped nuts, a little of the herb that's inside the food, sesame seeds, a little drizzle of olive oil, chili sauce, or even a spoonful of salsa—assuming it works with the recipe.

- And for a dessert—a dusting of either powdered sugar or powdered cocoa will make anything look amazing.

The goal is simple: make it look nice. But as important as a little color on top is, please don't garnish with something just for color. Only use things that actually go with the dish. The simply great Smoked Salmon Cream Cheese Omelet on page 86 has no business with cilantro or parsley on top of it. The pepper, yes, but nothing else.

IF YOU PLATE IT, THEY WILL EAT IT. . . ALL OF IT

There are two reasons why you should resist the temptation to put so much food on the plate that it's falling off the edge.

- It looks like hell.

- Whatever you put on there, someone will eat.

This is not really meant to be a lesson in healthy eating, but do we honestly need all that food? And if it's there, it's gonna get eaten. So take a page out of the fancy restaurant playbook and keep a lot of plate showing. It'll look better, and you or your guests just won't eat as much. And the days of having three things on the plate—some kind of protein, a vegetable, and a starch—are so over. I say you adopt the "two things on a plate" approach and junk the starch.

FIRST, A WORD ABOUT CONDIMENTS

The dictionary defines a condiment as "something used to enhance the flavor of food." And I love condiments, all of them. Pickles, mustards, relishes, mayos, sauces, vinegars, Asian ones, ketchup-y ones, powders, rubs, syrupy things, olives, sweet, hot, sour, etc.—they all rule. Why do you think God invented that skinny space on the inside of a refrigerator door? It's to give all those little bottles and jars of condiments a place to live. And in the world of cooking simply but still ending up with big flavors, there's nothing easier than grabbing a bottle and pouring. I say you collect a few and keep 'em on hand. What's a sauce, really? Does it go on top or underneath? Should it be served hot or is it better cold? Do you pour it, dip it, or stuff it? The answer is: it can be anything you want it to be.

"THE SMILE IS BECAUSE I'M CLEANING & I DON'T MIND IT. IF YOU'RE GOING TO COOK, THERE'S GOING TO BE STUFF TO CLEAN. THE SOONER YOU'RE GOOD WITH THAT, THE BETTER."

ASIAN BBQ SAUCE

Where to use: Anywhere, as on chicken, steak, or even that dry-as-toast turkey breast. This is even good as a dip or painted on some skewered and grilled shrimp or scallops.

Makes 1¼ cups

2 tablespoons soy sauce

1 cup hoisin sauce

1 to 2 teaspoons hot chili sauce, the Asian kind

Mix all the ingredients together in a small bowl.

SPICY BBQ SAUCE

Makes about 1 cup

1 cup BBQ sauce, nothing flavored, just good ol' plain BBQ
1 to 2 canned chipotle peppers, chopped fine

Mix the ingredients together in a small bowl.

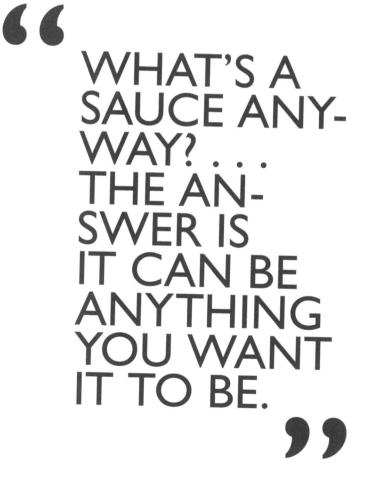

"WHAT'S A SAUCE ANY-WAY? . . . THE AN-SWER IS IT CAN BE ANYTHING YOU WANT IT TO BE."

PESTO

The classic combination of basil, olive oil, pine nuts, garlic, and Parmesan cheese is one of the most versatile things you can have in your fridge. And you could make your own, but any version you buy will be ridiculously close to what you'd make anyway. So trust me—don't make it, just buy it.

Here are a few ideas for what to do with pesto:

- Mix some with a little more olive oil and paint across the top of a steak that's just come off the grill and is still really hot— oh, my . . .

- Stuff a chicken breast with pesto and jarred roasted red peppers and then grill.

- Spread some on a pizza crust and then add the rest of the toppings.

- Mix some in with a little fresh pasta (see the Pasta section on page 167).

- Stir into baked or mashed potatoes.

- Add to any sandwich with turkey or chicken—it's all good.

- Brush a little on some veggies before grilling— incredible.

- Spoon a little on a piece of just-seared or grilled fish and add a drizzle of extra virgin olive oil.

- And it's amazing for garlic bread. Oh, wait, I just happen to have a recipe for that:

PESTO GARLIC BREAD

Really, does this need any kind of introduction?

Makes I baguette

- ¼ cup (½ stick) butter, softened
- ½ cup store-bought pesto
- ¼ cup shredded Parmesan cheese
- I long sourdough baguette

Turn the broiler to high.

In a small bowl, mix together the butter, pesto, and cheese well. Slice the baguette lengthwise and spread evenly with the pesto mixture.

Place 4 to 5 inches below the broiler until brown and bubbly, but not too brown. Remove from the oven, slice into 2-inch pieces, and serve—or run like hell to another room and eat it all by yourself.

SALSA CREAM

Where to use: This can be as simple as a little dip for veggies or chips, or it can be warmed and served on top of a grilled piece of fish or in the Fish (Stick) Tacos (page 228) or Fish (Stick) Burritos (page 229).

Makes 1½ cups

1 cup sour cream
½ cup green salsa

Mix together in a small bowl and serve cold, or mix in a small pot and heat slowly until warm.

"MOST THINGS YOU PUT ON A PLATE WILL LOOK WAY BETTER WITH A LITTLE SOMETHING ON TOP."

HONEY-MUSTARD SAUCE

Excuse me for boasting, but this is just one of those great, gooey amazing kind of things that make so many foods better.

Makes about 1½ cups

½ cup mayonnaise
1 tablespoon grainy mustard
1 tablespoon honey

Mix all the ingredients together in a small bowl.

ROASTED RED PEPPER SAUCE

Where to use: Amazing with pasta, fish, meat and even as a dip. In fact, you should just go ahead and make some now and keep it in the fridge—you'll be so glad you did.

Makes about 4 cups

- 1 12-ounce jar roasted red peppers, drained (I like the ones in oil—they just have more flavor)
- 1 28-ounce can whole peeled tomatoes
- 1 teaspoon crushed red pepper flakes

Put everything in a blender, and blend—pretty easy, huh? Then do this:

- Put some on a piece of grilled or seared fish—like this: Take a piece of fish (a fillet of some sort of white fish: cod, halibut, sea bass, mahi-mahi, etc.) and season it with some oil, kosher salt & fresh ground pepper. (BTW, I don't like a fish steak because it'll have all that bone structure in the middle.) Then heat a nonstick pan until almost smoking and put in the fish, which already has oil, so the pan shouldn't need any. It won't take more than about 5 minutes a side to get a good sear on it—and I even put a heavy little pan on top to help it sear the first side. And voilà . . . a little sauce on the bottom of the plate, then the fish, and a final drizzle of a good oil. Simple perfection.

- Spread a bunch on a sandwich as a layer to make everything better—think of it like mayo, but without the fat . . . and red instead of white and fewer calories. Okay, it's nothing like mayo—forget I even said that.

- Pour a little that's been heated on top of an over-easy egg that's on top of some grilled bread, then drizzle the whole thing with extra virgin olive oil. This is so crazy good you'll want to tell everyone about it.

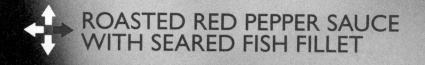

ROASTED RED PEPPER SAUCE
WITH SEARED FISH FILLET

SWEET CHILI SOY SAUCE

Where to use: As a dip for the Crab Won Tons on page 62. It's even great for a quick stir-fry sauce or simply drizzled on top of warm steamed white rice. Or try it as a dip for anything skewered.

You can just buy a bottle of sweet chili sauce—it's so good all by itself. But I like to add to it for just a tiny bit more joy . . .

Makes about ½ cup

½ cup sweet chili sauce (available in the supermarket's Asian section)

2 tablespoons soy sauce

3 green onions (scallions), thinly sliced (optional)

In a small bowl, mix together the chili sauce and soy sauce. If serving as a dipping sauce, put in a small serving dish and sprinkle with the green onions.

HORSERADISH, THE SAUCE

This is different from Horseradish, the Root—which I took a bite out of once. Talk about your basic huge-ass mistake. Anyway the jarred, grainy prepared root is good just like it is on brisket, that most delicious and Jewish of holiday foods. But when it comes to other things, there's two ways I like it: on a sandwich or burger (or any kinda bread or bun thing) or with a steak.

For a sandwich
Makes about ½ cup

  1 tablespoon prepared
     horseradish, the jarred kind
  ½ cup mayonnaise
  1 teaspoon olive oil
  Freshly ground black pepper

For a steak
Makes about ½ cup

  1 tablespoon prepared
     horseradish, the jarred kind
  ½ cup sour cream
  1 teaspoon olive oil
  Freshly ground black pepper

for a sandwich
A roast beef or turkey sandwich with this sauce is so unbelievable, I can't eat one without it.

Mix all the ingredients together in a small bowl and spread on your sandwich.

for a steak
Served on the side of a steak, this is killer.

Mix all the ingredients together in a small bowl and serve.

WASABI MAYO

Almost anywhere you use regular mayo, you can also use this wasabi version: sandwich, deviled eggs, chicken salad, for artichokes . . . get it?

Makes about ½ cup

½ cup mayonnaise
2 teaspoons prepared wasabi

In a small bowl, mix the ingredients together.

note

The key here is to snag a couple extra packets of wasabi the next time you get take-out sushi.

CHIPOTLE MAYO

Where to use: You put some of this with The Amazing Meatloaf Sandwich on page 146 and you'll almost be guaranteed a place in heaven. And don't feel left out, I don't even know what that's supposed to mean.

Makes about 1 cup

½ cup mayonnaise
2 canned chipotle chiles in adobo sauce, chopped fine

Mix the ingredients together in a small bowl.

note

Chipotle's are simply smoked jalapeños. I buy them at the supermarket in a can with adobo sauce. Think sort of a smoky and spicy bbq sauce—it's really good. You can use the chilies, the sauce, or both in recipes.

I've always felt that food is a full body experience (but not like that scene from *9½ Weeks* . . . in front of an open fridge . . . rubbing chocolate sauce and lasagna all over your body). So the following are simple little things to eat mostly with your fingers—though I'd probably put the Bacon Guacamole on something. It can get a little messy.

THINGS TO EAT WITH YOUR FINGERS

- simple won ton crackers

- corn, jalapeño & cheese biscuits

- sesame won ton crackers

- pancetta-grilled asparagus

- anything on skewers

- bacon guacamole

- crab won tons
- king crab legs

- asian wings

- blue cheese & bacon-stuffed dates

- red pepper & blue cheese bruschetta

- cap'n crunch seared tuna

SIMPLE WON TON CRACKERS

The problem with many store-bought crackers is that they often have additional flavor that you might not want. These are perfect because they let the dip part speak for itself. And when it comes to needing something crunchy for serving something not crunchy on, these are perfect. I really could have written that sentence better.

Makes as many as you need

Won ton wrappers—the square ones are approximately 4x4 inches (and there are about 50 in a pack), or the round ones, about 3 inches in diameter

Preheat the oven to 300°F.

Leave the round ones as is, or if using square ones, cut the wrappers down the middle to make them approximatley 2 x 4 inches and place in a single layer on an ungreased baking sheet. Bake for about 15 minutes, or until just beginning to brown.

note

If you can't find the square or round won ton wrappers, then buy the larger egg roll/ spring roll ones and cut them down. It's no big deal.

CORN, JALAPEÑO & CHEESE BISCUITS

Don't like the jalapeño heat? You could leave them out, but I wouldn't. I think it's time to start appreciating new flavors—just try a little less of them.

Makes about 18

1½ cups Bisquick
1 tablespoon diced jalapeño
1 8-ounce can creamed corn
½ cup shredded cheddar cheese

Preheat the oven to 400°F. Lightly butter a large baking sheet.

Mix all the ingredients together in a large bowl.

Drop tablespoons of the batter onto the baking sheet about 3 inches apart.

Bake until lightly golden, about 20 minutes.

Serve them warm if you can, but if not, no big deal—in fact they're great room temp at an outdoor kind of thing.

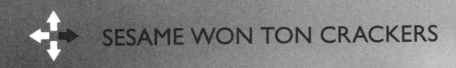

SESAME WON TON CRACKERS

SESAME WON TON CRACKERS

Only two things make this more complicated than the simple ones.

Makes as many as you need

Won ton wrappers
Sesame oil
Sesame seeds, white, black or both

Preheat the oven to 300°F.

Leave the round ones as is, or if using square ones, cut the wrappers down the middle to make them approximatley 2 x 4 inches and place in a single layer on an ungreased baking sheet. Brush with sesame oil and then sprinkle with seeds. Bake for about 15 minutes, or until just beginning to brown.

PANCETTA-GRILLED ASPARAGUS

PANCETTA-GRILLED ASPARAGUS

Pancetta is really just Italian bacon— and I know it sounds like I'm getting all fancy on you, but I'm not. If you can buy packaged salami in the store, you can buy this. But referring to it as pancetta and not bacon will make you feel more worldly.

Makes about 15

1 pound fresh asparagus
6 ounces pancetta, cut lengthwise

Trim the bottom inch from each asparagus spear. Wrap each stalk all the way around with the pancetta from just below the cool head part to the bottom.

Place on a medium-high grill, grill pan, or under the broiler. Cook until the asparagus has softened and the pancetta starts getting a bit crispy on the edges.

ANYTHING ON SKEWERS

I don't want this to be seen as a throwaway section, because I feel strongly about this as an entertaining option. Not only is it fun for your guests to grill these things themselves, but because they're doing part of the work, you can be doing something else. It's really as simple as skewering anything, and the beautiful thing is, it doesn't have to be on a BBQ. You can easily do this in your kitchen on a grill pan.

Buy Wooden or Metal Skewers

If you use wood, soak them in a large glass of water about 30 minutes before putting food on them so they don't burn while you are grilling.

Skewer One or Two Bite-Sized Pieces of Anything on the End

This can be a piece of chicken, beef, sausage, veggie, a chunk of baguette (that's really good), or even fruit in the summer, such as cut-up pineapple or peach. But only put a couple of bites on each stick. It'll look better and your guests won't run the risk of skewering their tonsils.

Mix and Match Things

A piece of beef with a piece of green onion or even a hunk of chicken with some pineapple. I know I said I wouldn't mention anything that's crazy to find, but there's a cheese called halloumi that won't melt on the grill—if you can find it, it's fun to use.

> **NOT ONLY IS IT FUN FOR YOUR GUESTS TO GRILL THESE THINGS THEMSELVES, BUT BECAUSE THEY'RE DOING PART OF THE WORK, YOU CAN BE DOING SOMETHING ELSE.**

Lay Them All Out with Sauces for Your Guests to Dip into

And they can dip before, during, or after the cooking. Certainly any store-bought Asian sauce will work—hoisin, black bean, and the BBQ ones are great too. Think about it: anything grilled is good by itself, so adding a little sauce just makes it even better.

And Then Give 'Em a Final Dip into . . .

Once the item is cooked, it can get a final tap into something for a little extra flavor: sesame seeds (white or black), some shredded Parmesan cheese, freshly ground black pepper, coconut flakes, panko bread crumbs, anything.

BACON GUACAMOLE

This is like a BLAT—bacon, lettuce, avocado, and tomato sandwich—but with the two things that are actually good for you (the lettuce & tomato) removed.

Where to use: anywhere guacamole goes—but don't forget how fantastic it is on a burger.

Makes about 2 cups

2   ripe avocados
½   cup chunky red salsa
2   ounces "ready" bacon, cooked
      crisp and crumbled
    Juice of ½ lime
    Pinch kosher salt

Spoon out the avocado flesh and put in a small bowl (I still can't get over calling it flesh). Mash it a bit with the back of a fork, but not too much.

Add the salsa, bacon, lime juice, and salt. Mix well and serve.

BACON GUACAMOLE

CRAB WON TONS

These fall under the heading of "Don't make the same thing all the time." They're delicious, simple, and different—plus they're baked, not fried. I would try to insist on fresh crab, but there's no point. You're going to use what you want, and besides, canned in this case is actually not that bad. But if you do use canned, buy the "lump" kind that's been pasteurized.

Makes about 30

4 ounces cream cheese, softened
1 cup crabmeat, approximately
3 green onions (scallions), the white and light green parts sliced very thin
1 tablespoon Asian hot sauce (Sriracha®)
1 package won ton wrappers—I like the round ones
½ cup Sweet Chili Soy Sauce (page 44)

Preheat the oven to 400°F. Lightly coat a baking sheet with cooking spray.

In a bowl, mix the cream cheese, crabmeat, green onions, and hot sauce together well.

Put about a teaspoon and a half of the mixture in the center of each wrapper. Wet the edges of the wrappers with a little water and fold in half—try to remove as much air as possible. Seal tightly and place on the baking sheet.

Bake until lightly browned, 15 to 20 minutes.

Serve with the Sweet Chili Soy Sauce on the side for dipping.

KING CRAB LEGS

This is a great opening to a romantic meal for two. Crab has a bit of a stigma of being a pain to cook—it's not.

Serves 2

¼ cup (½ stick) butter
I pound king crab legs, the already-cooked kind
½ teaspoon freshly ground pepper
½ teaspoon chili powder

Separate the butter into 2 small, microwaveable bowls—but don't do anything with them yet. I feel bad saying this, but break the crab legs into 5-to 6-inch-long pieces.

Fold 3 paper towels in half, so they're sort of 1½ paper towels long. Lightly dampen the towels with water, bundle the legs like firewood, then wrap the towels around the crab legs. Place the bundle in the microwave and cook on high for 2 minutes.

Remove the crab from the microwave and, while you're putting it onto a platter, put the butter bowls into the microwave to melt—about 30 seconds should do it.

Remove the bowls and add the pepper to one and the chili powder to the other. To serve, open the shells, get to the meat, and dip into your favorite butter sauce (but be sure to try both before you decide).

"I EAT A LOT OF FOOD IN MY KITCHEN —FOR TV, FOR RECIPE TESTING & OFTEN JUST FOR ME. AND MOST OF THE TIME IT'S SPENT OVER THE SINK, OR SHOULD BE. "

THE JO JO
(PAGE 112)

COME
INTO
MY
KITCHEN
& SEE
HOW
IT'S
DONE!

oil it

fill it

grill it

slice it

cream cheese

sprinkle it

WORLD'S BEST DESSERT WAFFLE
(PAGE 244)

drizzle.

add nuts

sprinkle & eat

RED PEPPER & BLUE CHEESE BRUSCHETTA (PAGE 68)

BLUE CHEESE GNOCCHI
WITH BACON (PAGE 178)

MEATBALL STROGANOFF
(PAGE 212)

THE MANEDICT
(PAGE 78)

CHIMICHITO
(PAGE 128)

BACON GUACAMOLE
(PAGE 60)

SAM'S MEXICAN MEATLOAF
(PAGE 142)

THE AMAZING MEATLOAF SANDWICH
(PAGE 146)

dice it

spread

add potatoes

cream cheese

a dab will do it

bite in & enjoy!

PANCETTA-GRILLED ASPARAGUS
(PAGE 57)

SHRIMP
(PAGE 197)

PEA SOUP
(PAGE 219)

CHEATER SEAFOOD PAELLA
(PAGE 192)

PULLED CHICKEN SANDWICH
(PAGE 123)

slice it

layer it

bite it

slice it

roll it

sear it

CAP'N CRUNCH SEARED TUNA
(PAGE 71)

plate it

ROASTED TOMATO PASTA
(PAGE 181)

ROASTED RED PEPPER SAUCE WITH SEARED FISH FILLET
(PAGE 42)

cool it

PEACH AND RASPBERRY COBBLER
(PAGE 241)

plate it

sprinkle

maybe better over the sink!

ASIAN WINGS

I always keep a bag of frozen chicken wings around.

Makes 24

- ¾ **cup soy sauce**
- ¾ **cup brown sugar**
- 24 **frozen chicken wings, defrosted—or fresh if you insist**
   Sesame seeds

Mix the soy sauce and brown sugar together well in a bowl.

Put the wings in a zipper-top plastic bag, add 1 cup of the sauce (reserving the rest for basting), coat well, and allow to marinate for up to a couple hours—but if you only have 5 minutes, go with that. Meanwhile, preheat the broiler.

Transfer to a baking sheet without the marinade. Place under the broiler for 15 minutes, or until golden brown, basting 2 or 3 times. Flip the wings and cook for another 15 minutes or so, basting again 2 or 3 times.

Serve on a platter and sprinkle with sesame seeds.

BLUE CHEESE & BACON–STUFFED DATES

Everything's working in concert here: You've got the sweet of the date, the savory of the blue cheese, and the salty of the bacon. This hits so many senses it's almost food in 3-D. BTW, that pretty much makes no sense.

Makes as many as you want

Pitted dates
Wedge of blue cheese, cut into ½-inch chunks, thin enough so they fit into the date hole
"Ready" bacon
Bamboo skewers

Preheat the oven to 450°F.

Snip open one side of the date with small kitchen shears. Stuff a cube of the cheese into a date and wrap the edges around it to cover the cheese.

Wrap each date one time around fairly snugly with bacon, trimming off the end if needed. Repeat with the remaining dates.

Skewer the bacon-wrapped dates, putting about 4 on each skewer. Place on a baking sheet and put in the oven for about 15 minutes, until the bacon is brown and crispy and the cheese is melting. Remove, let cool just slightly, and then eat.

note

Another option would be to cook them on a grill instead of in the oven.

RED PEPPER & BLUE CHEESE BRUSCHETTA

Once again, that jar of roasted red peppers comes to the rescue.

Makes 16 to 20 pieces

1 long thin sourdough baguette
  Olive oil
1 12-ounce jar roasted red
  peppers, drained well
4 ounces blue cheese crumbles

Preheat the oven to broil.

Cut the heels off the bread and slice in half lengthwise. Put on a baking sheet and drizzle lightly with the oil.

Place under the broiler until just getting crisp, maybe a minute.

Top the bread with the peppers and then the blue cheese crumbles.

Put back under the broiler to heat through and start to melt the cheese, a couple minutes. Cut diagonally into 2- to 3-inch pieces and serve.

CAP'N CRUNCH SEARED TUNA

CAP'N CRUNCH™ SEARED TUNA

note

As my editor Justin pointed out, this may not be finger food for everyone. Well, I say, maybe it should be. You'd eat a chicken tender with your fingers, right? So why not this? I mean, they're both coated in something and then cooked? And just because this one sounds silly doesn't mean you must have a fork. So maybe use chopsticks. Whatever you do, just make it. It's crazy good.

Serves 6 as an appetizer

¼ cup mayonnaise
1 tablespoon yellow mustard
2 cups regular Cap'n Crunch™ (don't even think of using the peanut butter or crunch-berry version)
2 tablespoons oil
1 pound fresh tuna, ideally cut into 2 long rectangular blocks
   Kosher salt and freshly ground pepper
   Asian chili sauce (Sriracha)
¼ cup finely diced green onions (scallions)

In a small bowl, mix the mayo and mustard together and set aside.

Put the cereal in a large zipper-top plastic bag and crush the hell out it—you want it like dust. Spread the crushed cereal on a large plate.

Lightly oil the tuna, season it with salt and pepper, then press down into the Cap'n Crunch™, making sure it's covered well on all sides.

Heat a nonstick pan really well first and then add about a table-spoon of oil. When the oil just starts to smoke, add the tuna and sear it quickly on all sides until lightly browned. If it's hot enough, you need probably no more than about 15 seconds a side.

Remove and carefully slice into ½-inch pieces.

To serve, spread the mayo mix on a plate, top that with the sliced tuna, and drizzle a bit of the chili paste around it. Sprinkle with the green onions. Make sure you have some of everything in each bite.

Look, if you haven't read my thoughts on "ingredients" in the Ground Rules chapter, you should. Because spending a lot of money on the tuna for this recipe would be a sin. But not nearly as big as not making it would be.

I'm convinced the title, "The Most Important Meal of the Day" was bestowed upon breakfast by a man, and no, I'm not being sexist. It's just that if there's one meal a man can make—it's this one. Ask any guy what he can cook, and some form of breakfast, especially one with eggs, will always be in the lineup. Why? I believe there are two reasons. The first, and most appropriate for our purposes, is that eggs are quick. If you can't go from raw to eating in less than 5 minutes, you've got issues. And the second, though mostly inappropriate, is that offering to make a woman "breakfast in the morning" definitely increases the chances of there being an "in the morning"—know what I mean? That said, there's no reason ever to limit breakfast to just in the morning. Have it whenever the feeling takes you.

MY FAVORITE MEAL— BREAKFAST

- smoked salmon cream cheese omelet

- crab omelet

- how to cook an over-easy egg the right way

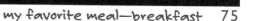

- chilaquiles

- the popeye

- cream cheese-&-jelly-stuffed french toast

While we're in breakfast, I want to share an important egg thing, the more-often-than-not screwed up . . .

HARDBOILED EGG

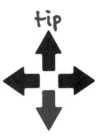

A properly hard-boiled egg should not have that creepy grey ring around the yolk. That comes from over cooking.

Makes as many as you want

> Eggs
> Cold water

Carefully put the eggs in a pot and add enough cold water to cover them by about an inch. I say "carefully" because if you're rough with the eggs, you can make a slight crack that will render them useless—so put them in gently, ya dig? Don't cover the pot.

Put over medium-high heat. Allow the water to come to a full boil and then let it boil for 2 minutes. Turn off the heat and cover with a lid. Leave for 10 more minutes.

Remove the lid, carefully pour off the very hot water, and refill with cold water and a lot of ice to stop the cooking. Refrigerate.

How is a hard-boiled egg breakfast, you're wondering? Well, how isn't it? It's great protein, and if you spike them with a little hot sauce while you're standing at the sink eating them . . . they're amazing.

And now that you've learned how to hard-boil an egg the right way—go make The Best Chicken/Egg Salad (page 125).

Egg Tip: A fresh egg that's been hard-boiled is more difficult to peel than an older egg that's been hard-boiled. So, if you can think ahead, buy your eggs a week or so before you need them. And if you do, you'll be a week ahead of me, because I never remember.

Someone's gotta clean up.

HOW TO POACH AN EGG & BECOME A BREAKFAST SUPERHERO

Now we come to the one breakfast thing that you can fake and still gain near-superstar status—the Benedict. One of the most revered (and expensive) breakfast items on any restaurant menu, it's merely a poached egg with stuff on it, under it or both. The real way to poach an egg can be difficult. So feel free to buy a microwave egg poacher, get a regular poacher pan thing, or use little metal cups in a pot of boiling water—this is what I do. I use a cup that essentially looks like a metal ½ cup measuring cup but has rounded edges inside. I butter it and crack an egg into it. Then I put that into a pot of almost-boiling water—but the water goes only about ¾ of the way up the sides of the cup. I put the lid on and leave it for about 90 seconds until the white is cooked but the yolk is still runny. Here's the deal—no matter how you get there, just get there, because with the egg and the packaged Hollandaise and gravy I told you to keep in your pantry, you can make these Benedicts:

Standard—English muffin, Canadian bacon, poached egg, Hollandaise

Smoked Salmon—English muffin, smoked salmon, poached egg, Hollandaise

The Chesapeake Bay—English muffin, avocado, poached egg, crab, Hollandaise, and a light sprinkle of Old Bay seasoning

The Manedict—Toasted bagel, thinly sliced leftover steak, poached egg, French fries, jarred gravy (with a couple shakes of Worcestershire sauce stirred into the gravy first)

There is just something so profoundly satisfying about making any kind of eggs Benedict that you'll end up standing on the counter of your kitchen screaming:

"I'M THE KING OF THE WORLD!!" UNLESS YOU'RE A WOMAN—THEN YOU CAN YELL, "I'M THE QUEEN OF THE WORLD!!"

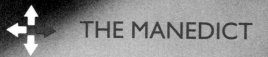

A WORD ABOUT PANCAKES

I love pancakes but never really get the urge to make them from scratch. Look, I can appreciate the person who does, I'm just saying, that's not me. So keeping a box of the "just add water" type pancake mix in my pantry makes having them whenever I want a snap.

Sometimes I like them plain, and sometimes I like them with stuff, for example:

Add-Ins
- Savory—diced cooked bacon, diced cooked ham, bits of chopped-up fully cooked sausage

- Sweet—chips (chocolate, butterscotch, etc.)— Not my bag, but go for it if you want.

- Crunchy—granola, Cap'n Crunch, cereal, nuts

- Fruity—berries—blue, straw, rasp, black— whatever works for you. Just make sure you dust the pancakes with powdered sugar (for extra flavor and a nice effect) before serving.

- Woodsy—maple Syrup—add 2 tablespoons to every 2 cups of powdered mix.

The key to using an add-in is to resist the urge to mix it in with the batter. Instead, simply drop it onto the batter once you've poured the pancake into the pan—unless you're making the Pecan Crunch Pancakes below . . .

Of course, you could do any of this with waffles, but I don't have a waffle iron and don't want one. It's not that I'm a waffle hater; it's just that I can make pancakes with pretty much any pan I already own. Waffles require a waffle iron, and the last thing I need is an extra piece of pain-in-the-ass equipment that I have to store somewhere and will only use once every 3 months. Actually, now that I think about it—I am a waffle hater.

And for pancakes with just a tad more work, try one of these two:

" I CAN MAKE PANCAKES WITH ANY PAN I ALREADY OWN. "

PECAN CRUNCH PANCAKES

If you dig the crunchy, sweet top of a pecan roll, you'll love this.

Makes 6 to 8 pancakes

- 1 cup "just add water" pancake mix
- 3 tablespoons butter
  Syrup, for serving
- ½ cup brown sugar
- 1 cup chopped pecan pieces

Prepare the pancake mix according to the package directions.

Heat a nonstick pan or griddle over medium-high heat.

Melt about a teaspoon of butter in a 4-inch circle in the pan.

Sprinkle 1 tablespoon of brown sugar on top of the butter.

Add pecans to the circle and cover with about ¼ cup of pancake batter. Cook until the bottom is nicely golden brown, then flip. Cook on the second side until done—the time will be way less.

Repeat with the remaining pancake batter, butter, sugar, and pecans. Serve hot with syrup.

PIÑA COLADA PANCAKES

It's just like the drink, except it's hot and flat.

Makes about 8 pancakes

- I cup "just add water" pancake mix
- ½ cup coconut milk
- ⅓ cup unsweetened coconut flakes
- ¼ cup water
- ¼ cup white rum
- Butter
- ½ cup diced pineapple
- Syrup, for serving

In a medium-sized bowl, combine the pancake mix, coconut milk, coconut flakes, water, and rum—mix well.

Heat a nonstick skillet or griddle over medium heat.

Melt some butter in the skillet and spoon 2 to 3 tablespoons of the batter into the pan to make small pancakes. Cook the pancakes until they are browned on one side and a bunch of bubbles appear on the surface, about 2 minutes, then flip and cook until the second side is nicely browned.

To serve, put some of the pineapple onto a plate and add a small stack of the pancakes next to it.

Drizzle the pancakes with syrup and eat away.

THE KAPLAN SPECIAL

If I ever opened a restaurant, this would absolutely for sure be on the breakfast menu. It's way old school from my mom's family, and I could eat it every day.

Serves 2

1 teaspoon olive oil
1 small yellow onion, sliced into thin strips
2 tomatoes, cored and cut into small wedges
2 tablespoons Worcestershire sauce
  Salt and pepper to taste
2 pieces bread, whatever works for you
2 large eggs
6 slices cooked bacon

Heat a medium pan and add the oil. Add the onion and cook, stirring, until starting to soften, about 5 minutes.

Add the tomatoes and cook, stirring, until they soften too, a couple more minutes. Add the Worcestershire and season to taste with salt and pepper. While that simmers slowly, toast the bread and fry the eggs (over easy, please).

To serve, place some of the onion/tomato mixture on a piece of toast, add an egg, and top with bacon.

SMOKED SALMON CREAM CHEESE OMELET

My mom used to make a cream cheese omelet, but we didn't have the smoked salmon version in those days—it hadn't been invented by a bagel store yet.

Makes I omelet

- 3 large eggs
- ½ teaspoon dried dill
  Kosher salt and freshly ground pepper to taste
- I tablespoon butter
- 2 ounces smoked salmon cream cheese, softened

In a bowl, season the eggs with the dill and salt and pepper to taste. Beat well.

Heat a nonstick skillet over medium heat. Add the butter and allow to melt and coat the pan.

Add the eggs and cook by pulling them away from the sides of the pan so the raw egg runs underneath to cook.

Once the eggs are about halfway set, add the cream cheese on one half of the omelet. Allow it to melt slightly, then fold the omelet over to form a half moon and let the eggs finish cooking.

Transfer to a plate and serve.

CRAB OMELET

Since we're in omelet world, allow me to present another fav—the crab version. This is made with canned crab, which can be really good. Look for the pasteurized kind.

Makes 1 omelet

1 teaspoon butter
2 tablespoons finely diced red bell pepper
2 large eggs
    Kosher salt and freshly ground black pepper to taste
⅓ cup lump crabmeat
2 tablespoons Monterey Jack cheese

Heat a nonstick skillet over medium heat.

Add the butter and the red pepper to the pan. Cook, stirring, until the red pepper is slightly softened.

Meanwhile, in a small bowl, beat the eggs well and add salt and pepper to taste.

Pour the eggs over the softened red bell pepper. Cook the eggs by pulling them away from the sides of the pan so the raw egg runs underneath to cook.

Once the egg is about halfway set, add your crab and cheese. Fold the omelet in half and continue to cook so that the crab heats in the center, the cheese gets melty, and the eggs finish cooking.

Transfer to a plate, sprinkle with a little more freshly ground pepper, and serve.

"DESPITE WHAT MY FACE IS SAYING, SHOOTING PICTURES FOR THIS BOOK WAS JUST A TON OF FUN. I LOOK SO SAD, DON'T I?"

contemplating the next shot

HOW TO COOK AN OVER-EASY EGG THE RIGHT WAY

So here I am writing this chapter and I come to the decision that I should try to teach people how to cook an over-easy egg without busting the yolk—because for over-easy people, it's all about the yolk. But the problem is . . . I instantly start a conversation in my own head about it. And here's how it goes, in the order it happens:

Me: People should know how to cook an egg over easy—I'll write about it.

Me: Wait, that's stupid—everyone already knows how.

Me: Yeah? So if they do, I wouldn't be getting asked all the time about how not to break the yolk.

Me: Fine. But maybe not everyone likes an over-easy egg.

Me: Well they should—the flavor's there.

Me: So you're going to force your love of runny egg yolks on them.

Me: Yup, guess so.

Me: It's your book, go ahead.

Me: Oh, don't you worry, I will.

So here you go:

OVER-EASY EGGS (THE "NOT-BROKEN-YOLK" WAY)

Heat a nonstick skillet over medium heat and add a little butter. When the butter stops foaming, crack your eggs into the pan and season with salt and pepper.

As the white part is starting to set, make sure to lightly loosen the edges with a spatula—you don't want any sticking. If any white part tries to escape, herd it back into an oval-ish egg shape.

Note: The key is not to flip too early.

So . . . once the whites are mostly set, which should be anywhere from about 45 seconds to a minute or so, take your spatula and, in one quick move, slide it completely under the egg and then gently flip it over.

Now it's only a matter of 15 to 30 seconds on that side until it's done.

There are plenty of people who'll tell you to do the "pan-and-wrist flip thing" when cooking eggs. But unless you've worked in a diner, that usually just results in broken yolks on your floor—and I hate when that happens.

tip

Another Egg Tip: Instead of frying your egg in butter, try cooking it in olive oil. It's pretty damn good.

CHILAQUILES

Fresh, crunchy tortilla chips are great. Stale ones from a bag that's been left open are not. This is a really easy version of the Mexican favorite that will give your "about-to-be-thrown-out" tortilla chips a new home, and it's dog simple. I like to make it in a Pyrex pie plate and add fried eggs on top. It's the perfect "late-night-after-being-out-partying" food, and also the perfect "morning-after-whatever" food. Talk about versatile . . .

Serves 4

1 cup green enchilada sauce
6 ounces tortilla chips
1 cup green salsa
1½ cups shredded Monterey Jack cheese
4 large eggs, optional—wait I take that back, they're not optional

In this order, cover the bottom of a glass pie plate first with half the enchilada sauce, then half the tortilla chips, then half the salsa, and then half the cheese.

Repeat to make the second layer with the remaining chips, enchilada sauce, salsa, and cheese.

Microwave for 5 minutes.

If you're going to, this is the time to cook the eggs. And I'd suggest over-easy eggs, as the runny yolk just makes the whole thing way better. But far be it for me to try to impose my food likes on you. Feel free to go with any style eggs you like (but the over-easy ones will just be better).

THE POPEYE

Also known as an "egg-in-the-hole," a "bird's nest," or a "ring-around-the-yolky," this classic is the greatest way ever invented to eat a piece of bread and a single egg.

Makes 1

1 piece of bread—rye or pumpernickel, for this is the best
Butter
1 large egg
Kosher salt and freshly ground pepper

Preheat a nonstick pan over medium heat.

Cut a hole 2 to 3 inches in diameter in the middle of the bread. Remove the cut out hole piece but don't throw it away—it's important.

Add some butter to the pan and add both pieces of bread. Allow them to brown on one side for about 1 minute.

Crack an egg in the center of the hole, season with the salt and pepper, and cook until the white sets.

Flip the egg-bread over and the cutout circle—of course be careful not to break the yolk—and finish cooking until it's the way you like it.

Serve and use the center piece of bread for dipping in the yolk.

CREAM CHEESE-&-JELLY–STUFFED FRENCH TOAST

Once you learn the key, you can stuff bread with anything . . .

Makes 4 pieces

- 2 3-inch-thick slices bread (challah, the doughy egg bread of my people, is ideal)
- 4 big tablespoons softened cream cheese
- 4 big tablespoons jelly (I like grape)
- 2 large eggs, beaten
- 1 tablespoon milk
  Butter
  Powdered sugar

Cut a horizontal opening in one side of each slice of bread to make a pocket—but don't cut all the way through. Spread some cream cheese and jelly inside each pocket.

In a shallow, medium-sized bowl, beat the eggs with the milk.

Heat a nonstick skillet over medium heat and add butter. Once the butter has melted, dip each stuffed-bread deal into the egg mixture (be sure to cover both sides AND the ends) and place in the pan.

Cook for 3 to 4 minutes on each side until golden brown—cook the fat edges too.

To serve, put on a plate and sprinkle with a little powdered sugar.

CREAM CHEESE-&-JELLY–STUFFED
FRENCH TOAST

This lunchtime combo seems like such a good idea. Why hasn't it caught on at other mealtimes? I mean, the possibilities are really endless . . . bacon or sausages with half an egg Benedict? Steak or shrimp with half a lasagna? Sorbet or ice cream with half a crème brûlée? Having to choose at lunch seems okay, but I think the problem is people don't want to have to decide at other mealtimes as well. In fact, I want the sausage, bacon, half a Benedict with a side of steak, the shrimp, lasagna, and crème brûlée topped with sorbet ice cream all at one meal.

SOUP OR SALAD WITH HALF A SANDWICH

- focaccia

- five-minute beer bread

- chili cornbread with honey butter

- baby caprese salad

- chopped greek panzanella salad

- bbq cole slaw

- two-minute roasted tomato basil soup

- my big fat greek avgolemono soup

- thai curry noodle soup

- the jojo

- pesto, shrimp and white bean soup

- antipasto sandwich

FOCACCIA

Focaccia is sort of a flat oven-baked Italian bread that you can top with herbs or other ingredients." Okay, so this one starts out life as a tube of refrigerated pizza dough, who cares? The only thing that matters is the end product. Think chewy, fragrant, warm, and delicious. You okay now? Slice it in half and make something out of it.

Makes 10 to 12 pieces

1   14-ounce tube refrigerated
     pizza dough
1   tablespoon olive oil
½ cup pitted kalamata olives,
     roughly chopped
2   tablespoons shredded
     Parmesan cheese
½ teaspoon dried rosemary
     Pinch of kosher salt

Preheat the oven to 400°F. Spray a baking sheet with cooking spray or line it with parchment.

Open the tube, then unroll and place the dough on the baking sheet. Try to press it out to about ½ inch thick.

Drizzle the dough with the olive oil. Evenly scatter the olives, Parmesan, rosemary, and a pinch of salt over the top. Take the pads of your fingers and lightly push the toppings down a bit. Bake for about 20 minutes, until the dough is cooked through but not too browned.

Slice into pieces and serve with anything.

FIVE-MINUTE BEER BREAD

I can remember being ten years old, walking down the lane to Chucky Diamond's house and being able to smell the fresh bread his mom was baking—incredible still. But no light, wispy, and airy little breads for me. I like a heavy, dense loaf, still warm with butter. Plus, you make this in about 5 minutes—what could be better? And talk about sandwiches . . .

Makes 1 totally bitchin' loaf

- 3 cups self-rising flour
- 3 tablespoons sugar
- 1 12-ounce bottle medium-dark beer, at room temperature

Preheat the oven to 350°F. Grease a loaf pan.

In a large bowl, mix together the flour and sugar, then slowly stir in the beer. Mix everything until it is smooth.

Place in the loaf pan and put the pan in the center of the oven. Bake for about 50 minutes. Remove from the oven and take the bread out of the pan. Allow to cool on a rack or the grates of your stovetop.

Slice, butter, and serve warm.

CHILI CORNBREAD WITH HONEY BUTTER

"Just add water" cornbread mix and plain ol' chili powder make a great and simple combo. And the honey butter . . . well, that just speaks for itself.

Serves 10

1 package cornbread mix
2 tablespoons chili powder
1 tablespoon honey
¼ cup butter, softened

Mix the cornbread according to package instructions. Stir in the chili powder, pour into the pan, and bake according to package instructions. While it cooks, stir the honey into the butter and set aside.

I SHOULDN'T HAVE TO DESCRIBE WHAT TO DO NEXT, SHOULD I?

BABY CAPRESE SALAD

This is pretty much a one-ingredient salad dressing—just really good olive oil. And the whole thing is not just really simple, it's really impressive. I think this baby version kicks ass over all the other ones.

Serves 4

10 ounces baby tomatoes, the little cherry kind (try to get both red and yellow)
1 tub (about 8 ounces) fresh small mozzarella balls (called bocconcini)
 About 8 basil leaves, torn or cut into smallish pieces
2 tablespoons extra virgin olive oil
 Kosher salt and freshly ground black pepper

Slice the tomatoes and cheese balls in half and put in a bowl. Add basil. Drizzle with oil. Season with salt and pepper— don't be shy.

Mix and serve.

In the world of simple cooking and eating, this salad with a steak or a piece of grilled chicken or fish doesn't get much better or easier. Or for a slightly more complex dressing, try extra virgin olive oil and a tablespoon of fresh lemon juice or some balsamic vinegar . . . it's so amazing.

> "KELLY IS MY TOTAL FOOD OPPOSITE. SHE COULD EAT ONLY SALAD FOR THE REST OF HER LIFE & BE HAPPY. IF I NEVER ATE SALAD FOR THE REST OF MY LIFE, I'D BE HAPPY."

CHOPPED GREEK PANZANELLA SALAD

Panzanella is an Italian salad that uses stale bread. I'm not a big salad guy, but this one I could eat every day. It's worth making sure you have leftover bread to use. I'm also not big on making my own salad dressings—but I like to make this one.

Serves 4

SALAD
- 4 medium-sized ripe tomatoes, diced small
- ½ medium red onion, diced small
- ½ cup kalamata olives, pitted and diced small
- 1 medium cucumber, peeled and diced small
- 6 ounces feta cheese, crumbled
- ½ loaf day-old sourdough bread, cut into ½-inch chunks

DRESSING
- ½ cup olive oil
- ¼ cup red wine vinegar
- 1 teaspoon dried oregano
- 2 teaspoons sugar

greek salad

Greek or Italian salad dressing—bottled or make the one below

In a large bowl, combine the veggies, most of the cheese, and bread.

Add the dressing, pouring on enough to coat everything. Let sit for 5 to 10 minutes, stirring occasionally.

Put on plates and serve with a little more feta crumbled over the top.

greek salad dressing

Big pinch kosher salt and freshly ground black pepper

Mix everything together in a container; cover and refrigerate.

BBQ COLE SLAW

This might sound weird, but it's really good. Put it on the side or, even better, on a burger or grilled chicken sandwich.

Serves 4

1 11-ounce bag "ready-to-go" coleslaw—the kit that also has the slaw sauce pack in it
⅓ cup barbeque sauce
2 teaspoons white vinegar

In a large bowl, mix together all the ingredients, including the sauce. Serve.

TWO-MINUTE ROASTED TOMATO BASIL SOUP

Warm or cold, a couple cans of tomatoes in the pantry make this soup a snap. Think about grilling a little bread to throw on the side. The focaccia on page 100 would be perfect.

Serves 4

1 28-ounce can roasted
 tomatoes with garlic
½ small yellow onion, rough
 chopped
1 small bunch fresh basil, about
 an ounce
 Kosher salt and freshly ground
 black pepper to taste—but
 don't be stingy
 Sour cream, for garnish

Put the tomatoes, onion, basil, and salt and pepper in a blender, but hold back a couple basil leaves. Blend, but not too fine—a little bit chunky is good. If you want to warm it up, now's the time.

Serve with some chopped basil and a little sour cream.

MY BIG FAT GREEK AVGOLEMONO SOUP

This is a wonderful little Greek rice and lemon soup that reminds me of Mrs. Poulos, the wonderful little Greek woman who used to make it for me.

Serves 4

4 cups chicken broth
½ cup rice
    Pinch of kosher salt
2 eggs, beaten
    Juice of 2 lemons
    Chopped parsley, for garnish

In a medium pot, bring the chicken broth to a boil, add the rice, and salt and turn down to a simmer for about 15 minutes.

In a medium bowl, beat the eggs and add the lemon juice.

This next part is key—if you just pour the egg mix into the soup right now it'll become Egg Drop Soup, which was in my last book, so don't. Take about a cup of the hot broth and slowly stir it into the beaten eggs.

Now that the egg mix is warmed up, you can add it back into the broth in the pot. Continue simmering until it thickens and is heated through and that's it. Serve with a little chopped parsley on top.

Eat your soup and throw your bowls in the fireplace when you're done. Okay, at the risk of having you ruin a bunch of your bowls, you should know I was only kidding about the throwing part. (Actually, I wasn't the one who was worried about this—it was my editor, Justin. He's a bit of a worrier.)

THAI CURRY NOODLE SOUP

All of this is off the shelf, except the shrimp, but even that can come right out of the freezer. If you can't make this at any time of any day, you aren't using this book properly.

Serves 4

2 cups chicken broth
1 14-ounce can coconut milk
½ tablespoon curry powder
½ tablespoon Asian chili paste
2 packs ramen noodles, without the seasoning pack
¾ pound raw shrimp, shelled and deveined
Green onions (scallions), cilantro, and limes, for garnish

Mix the broth, coconut milk, curry powder, and chili sauce in a medium pot and bring to a boil.

Turn down to a simmer and add the noodles and shrimp. In about 4 minutes, the noodles will be soft, the shrimp will be pink and cooked, and you'll be eating like Thai royalty.

Be sure to garnish with some green onions, cilantro, and a squeeze of lime.

THE JO JO

My middle son Jordan loves to cook, and this is easily one of his favorites.

Serves 1

Butter
1 large egg
Kosher salt and freshly ground black pepper to taste
2 ounces deli-sliced turkey
2 slices Gouda cheese (smoked is really good)
Mayonnaise
1 bagel, sliced in half and toasted
Avocado, enough to cover the bagel
Thinly sliced cucumber, enough to cover the bagel

Heat a nonstick skillet over medium heat. Melt some butter and crack the egg into the pan (break the yolk). Season with a little salt and pepper.

Place slices of turkey breast on the other side of the pan to heat through. When you flip the egg to cook the second side, top with the cheese to melt. Spread a little mayo onto the toasted bagel and add everything else in this order—sliced avocado, cucumber slices, grilled turkey, fried egg, and finally top with the other bagel half.

THE JO JO

PESTO, SHRIMP, AND WHITE BEAN SOUP

This feels very Italian countryside to me. I've never been to Italy, but if I went I would want this.

Serves 4

- 4 cups chicken broth
- 2 15-ounce cans cannellini beans, drained and rinsed
- ½ cup pesto
- 1 pound raw shrimp, shelled and deveined

Mix the broth, beans, and pesto together in a medium pot and bring to a simmer.

Add the shrimp and let simmer until cooked through, about 5 minutes. Serve.

ANTIPASTO SANDWICH

Everyone loves antipasto salad, right? Cured meats, olives, roasted garlic, artichoke hearts, cheeses, etc. Well, this is the sandwich version, and it's easy because a bunch of it comes out of a jar. Tapenade is simply an olive spread—any supermarket condiment aisle will have it.

Serves 2

⅓ cup "ready-made" olive tapenade
1 large crusty Italian roll, cut hot dog style leaving a "hinge"
12 slices deli salami
3 or 4 slices mozzarella cheese
5 ounces jarred marinated artichoke hearts, drained and roughly chopped
Fresh basil leaves

Spread the olive tapenade onto the roll. Cover with the salami. Add the cheese.

Cover with the artichoke hearts and basil leaves. Close the sandwich, cut in half, and share.

In my first book, I called the deli-roasted chicken one of the "best things in a supermarket these days." I don't believe that anymore. I now believe it's one of the best things, PERIOD. My father would call something of this caliber the "greatest thing since mother's milk." Have I mentioned my father's way with words? No? Well, you should hear him talk about something he doesn't like. Anyway, I love a rotisserie chicken—and they go into a trillion things:

- A handful of shredded chicken added to some soup (even canned soup)— makes almost any soup better.

- Sliced and added to a bag of "ready" Caesar salad to make a Chicken Caesar, duh . . .

- Cooked with a little onion and put in a taco.

- Mix some shredded chicken with a little cheese and salsa for an enchilada.

- Have I said just sliced and put in a chicken sandwich?

- Folded in a wrap with some fresh Bibb-lettuce and tomato.

- How about for a quesadilla?

- Stuffed in some "ready pie dough" circles with leftover mashed potatoes, then baked.

- Added to pretty much anything and on top of a pizza.

But maybe you want more than just ideas. Try these:

THE DELI-ROASTED CHICKEN

- chicken & pesto-stuffed biscuits

- inside-out grilled cheese

- pulled chicken sandwich

- chicken & bacon pot pie

- the best chicken/egg salad

- spicy chinese chicken pizza

- chimichito

CHICKEN & PESTO–STUFFED BISCUITS

You're basically making your own version of those microwaveable "pocket" things. And you know exactly what I'm talking about here, but I don't dare risk using the real name and having a limo full of attorneys pull up in front of my house with papers for me. The beauty is you simply make them anytime you want and with anything you want. In fact, the more creative you get, the better they get.

Makes 8

- 1 16-ounce tube large-sized refrigerator biscuits
- ¼ cup soft goat cheese
- ¼ cup store-bought pesto
- 1 cup shredded cooked chicken (from a precooked deli-roasted chicken)

Preheat the oven to 350°F. Lightly grease a baking sheet.

Remove the biscuits from the package and flatten into 4-inch circles.

Spread about 1 teaspoon each of the goat cheese and pesto in the center of each biscuit.

Top with some of the chicken, fold the biscuit over, and pinch the edges tight to form a half-moon.

Pierce each biscuit top 2 or 3 times with the point of a small knife and place on the baking sheet.

Bake for about 25 minutes, or until golden brown.

But here's the really beautiful thing—now that you've learned how to stuff them—you can stuff them with anything. For example:

- Diced-up roast beef, provolone cheese, and BBQ sauce
- Spaghetti sauce, pepperoni, and mozzarella cheese
- Tuna, a little spicy mayo, and some cheddar cheese
- Pastrami, grainy mustard, and Swiss cheese
- Peach pie filling
- Last night's roasted vegetables and feta cheese

You get the idea, right? My son Jordan calls them "Sam Pockets"—I'm so honored . . .

A fun thing to do is have a bunch of ingredients out, and let your family or guests build them the way the like . . . it's like a "pocket party."

INSIDE-OUT GRILLED CHEESE

Without sliced bread in the house one day and my boys asking for an ASGC (after-school grilled cheese), I was forced to punt and improvised with those little Hawaiian rolls. The inside-out part is you cook them inside out so you get a flat surface . . . you'll see.

BTW, I love Hawaiian rolls.

Makes 6 slider-sized sandwiches

1 package 6 Hawaiian sweet rolls, kept together as a 2 x 3 set
4 slices cheese—I'm cool with American slices, havarti, or anything that melts really well
1 cup shredded cooked chicken (from a precooked deli-roasted chicken)
6 pieces of "ready" bacon, cooked until crispy
Butter
Mustard

Preheat a large nonstick skillet over medium heat.

Cut the rolls (still connected together) horizontally in half so you have 2 big halves—you will use these inside out.

Cover half of the bread (you're covering the tops of the rolls) with half of the cheese and then with the chicken. Cover the chicken with the bacon and then the remaining cheese.

Put the other piece of bread on top (top down).

Butter the outside of the bread and cook until beautifully golden brown on each side.

Cut into 6 pieces (the size of the rolls) and serve with a little mustard on the side for dipping.

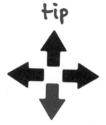

tip

What was the shortcut with using Hawaiian rolls, you wonder? It wasn't really a shortcut. It was a tip and I'll spell it out for you: Use what you've got. There's no law that says a grilled cheese has to be on regular sandwich bread—so try any of these: croissants, bagels, or whole baguettes, sliced lengthwise and grilled inside out like the recipe above.

PULLED CHICKEN SANDWICH

PULLED CHICKEN SANDWICH

This is a shortcut on the basic pulled pork sandwich, which, as it turns out, isn't so basic because it takes many hours of cooking. And whatever you do—do NOT leave out the onion rings.

Serves 6

3 cups shredded cooked chicken (from a precooked deli-roasted chicken)

¾ cup BBQ sauce

2 tablespoons white vinegar

6 good crusty rolls

2 cups "ready-to-go" coleslaw mix with dressing, prepared according to the package directions

18 frozen onion rings, cooked according to the package directions

In a small bowl, mix the chicken, BBQ sauce, and vinegar together and set aside.

Cut open the rolls, add some of the chicken mixture and coleslaw, then top each with a few of the warm onion rings—it's messy, but you're gonna love it.

Onion Ring Shortcut: Rather than cooking the frozen onion rings according to the package directions (slowly on bake), speed up the whole process by giving them a quick zap in the microwave and then cooking them under the broiler. Turn the rings over when one side is browned and cook the second side. They cook quickly—but that's what you want, right?

CHICKEN & BACON POT PIE

Just like Grandma's, but it has bacon and is made in about 10 minutes because of the jarred gravy, deli-roasted chicken, and "ready-made" pie crust you already had. The shortcut is using sour cream and jarred gravy instead of making your own roux (a mix of butter and flour used to thicken sauces).

Serves 10

- 1 teaspoon oil
- 8 ounces sliced mushrooms
- 1 small yellow onion, diced
- 3 cups cubed or shredded cooked chicken (from a precooked deli-roasted chicken)
- 1 cup sour cream
- 1 cup chicken gravy
- 1 tablespoon Worcestershire sauce
- 1 teaspoon dried thyme
- 1 "ready-made" pie crust

Preheat the oven to 425°F.

Heat a medium pan over medium heat. Add the oil, then add the mushrooms and onion and cook, stirring, until both are softened.

Add the chicken, sour cream, gravy, Worcestershire, and thyme and mix well.

Pour everything into a 9 x 9-inch baking dish and cover with the pie crust. Poke 6 small slits in the crust and bake for 30 to 40 minutes, or until golden brown.

THE BEST CHICKEN/EGG SALAD

This was born while I was looking for "something extra" to put in some egg salad I was making one day. I opened the fridge and saw someone had eaten almost all of the leftover chicken I put on a plate from the night before. I say "almost" because they left just enough to ensure they wouldn't have to deal with the empty dirty plate— you've been there, right? The chicken would have been useless for anything else, so I chopped it up and put it in with the eggs.

Try it open-faced on a toasted bagel. Holy-itshay . . .

Serves 4 to 6

6 large hard-boiled eggs, peeled
2 celery stalks, diced small
  (about ½ cup)
⅓ cup mayonnaise
2 cups shredded cooked chicken
  (from a precooked
  deli-roasted chicken)
2 teaspoons curry powder
  Freshly ground black pepper to
  taste

In a bowl, use a fork to roughly chop the eggs.

Add the celery, mayo, chicken, curry powder, and then pepper to taste. Mix together well and serve.

SPICY CHINESE CHICKEN PIZZA

You're going to like this a lot. Sweet, spicy, Asiany—it has it all. Hoisin is the best, and is easily bought at a supermarket.

Makes one 10-inch pizza

⅓ cup hoisin sauce
2 teaspoons chili paste, the Asian spicy kind
1 10-inch prebaked pizza crust
2 cups cooked shredded chicken
⅓ cup finely chopped green onions (white and light green parts)
½ cup shredded mozzarella
Chopped cilantro, for garnish

Preheat the oven to 425°F.

In a small bowl, mix together the hoisin and chili paste and spread it on the pizza crust. Place the chicken and green onions on the pizza and top with the cheese.

Bake 12 to 15 minutes, or until golden. Sprinkle with cilantro and cut into serving wedges.

CHIMICHITO

This is essentially a cross between a burrito and a chimichanga: all the good-filling-junk of a burrito and the crispiness of a chimichanga, but with none of the deep-frying pain-in-the-ass part.

Makes 4

- 3 cups shredded cooked chicken
- 1 cup jarred red salsa, the chunkier the better
- 1 4-ounce can diced green chilies
- 4 flour tortillas, burrito size
- 1 tablespoon oil
- 1 cup jarred red enchilada sauce
  Shredded cheddar cheese, sour cream, and cilantro, for garnish

Preheat the oven to 400°F. Lightly grease a baking sheet.

In a mixing bowl, combine the chicken, salsa, and green chiles and mix well.

Heat the tortillas a little just to make them pliable—I use a dry nonstick skillet, but even the microwave will work.

Spoon some of the chicken mixture on each tortilla. Roll them up, burrito-style—bottom over the mixture, sides in, and then roll away from you.

Place on the baking sheet and rub the top of the burritos lightly with oil. Bake until golden brown, about 20 minutes.

While they cook, heat the enchilada sauce in a separate small pot or in a bowl in the microwave.

To serve, spoon warm enchilada sauce on a plate, lay a chimichito on top, add a spoonful of sour cream, and sprinkle with cheese and cilantro.

At all food levels, you'll find meat and potatoes. From the basic burger and fries, to a rib eye with blue cheese mash, to a cilantro-crusted prime rib with roasted fingerlings (a weird finger-shaped potato) — but it's all just meat and potatoes. And when it comes to leftovers, not much beats them.

But we need to start someplace, so we'll start here:

MEAT & POTATOES
(MAKE GREAT LEFTOVERS)

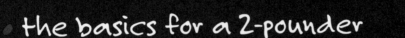

MEAT—SEASON SIMPLY

I might be weird, but generally I like meat to taste like, well, meat. And so my favorite and simplest way to cook a steak or something similar is to season only with kosher salt and freshly ground black pepper. I wrote about the importance of both of those in my first book, but let me say it this way: Using plain salt and plain shaker pepper will give you an okay steak, but not a great one. It's like asking your grandmother to run the hundred meters. She could do it, but it just wouldn't be all that exciting. But using kosher salt and freshly ground black pepper. . . now, that makes it exciting.

" AS SIMPLE AS IT GETS. "

MEAT—COOK SIMPLY

No advice here other than: don't go overboard—less is really more.

Heat a grill, pan, or broiler until very hot, and then add whatever it is that you're cooking. The key is lots of heat and a little time. You can always put something back to have it cook more, but you can't undo an overcooked piece of meat. I rarely cook a steak more than about 5 minutes a side—even a thick one. You can always make a small cut to see how done it is, but that's not ideal—it's a shame to let the juices out prematurely. This poke method will help you determine doneness. What works on your hand, works on the meat—trust me:

• Make a circle (as in the okay sign) with your thumb and forefinger. Don't tense, just make a circle. Then lightly push against the fat pad under the thumb of that circle with a finger from your other hand. This amount of squishiness generally represents a piece of meat that is rare.

• Now make that circle using your thumb and middle finger. And once again lightly push against the fat pad with a finger from your other hand. This amount of squishiness now will be close to representing a piece of meat that is medium rare.

• And finally, use the same system but this time, you guessed it—with the thumb and ring finger. And when you push against the fat pad under the thumb it will represent well done. But if you take anything away from this chapter, let it be this: never let it get well done. I'm sure I'll annoy a bunch of people, but there's just so much more flavor in anything other than well done.

Two more things to remember:

• Don't cook your meat cold—there's just no way for the outside and inside to cook properly if the inside is ice cold. So let it come to room temperature first—just take it out and leave it on the counter for about 30 minutes. Nothing bad will happen.

• And don't make the same thing over and over. There are all kinds of good cuts of meat, and I say you try a different cut each time you go to the market, just so you know what else is out there.

Now that we covered that part, how about some simple ideas?

COOK ONCE & EAT A COUPLE OF TIMES

An easy thing to do when cooking some meat is to just make a little extra. Just get an extra steak or two, or buy a larger cut. And it doesn't have to be the same cut. Let's say your plan is to grill a couple of rib eyes for dinner—pick up something less expensive and cook it at the same time. Then you can use it for all these things:

Steak Rice Bowls: Quickly stir-fry sliced steak with sliced red bell pepper and a little teriyaki sauce, then serve over white rice or brown rice.

Your Basic Steak Salad, of Course: One of the great gifts to mankind from, well, I have no clue, but it's easily my favorite salad. Sliced steak, tomatoes, cukes, some blue cheese crumbles, cooked beets, and almost any dressing and you'll be a genius. Don't forget lots of freshly ground pepper.

The Manedict: See the Breakfast chapter, page 78.

Philly Cheese Steak: Sliced green bell peppers and onions cooked in a hot pan . . . throw in the sliced steak, mix, then put some cheese slices on top. Let it all melt and then put the whole thing on a bun.

Steak French Dip: Okay, so maybe a real French dip is made with roast beef, but this one still kills. And all you need is a crusty roll and a package of instant "au jus" sauce for dipping.

Steak Tacos: Cook some sliced onions and add the sliced steak. Add a little cumin or chili powder, and put it on a tortilla with a little sour cream and anything else you need to use up—lettuce, cheese . . . you get it.

Shepherd's Pie: Despite what the shepherds were supposedly doing in the fields, they somehow found time to make a darn good pie (see page 158).

MEATLOAF 101

When it comes to meat one of the greatest things ever is a meatloaf. I love its diner-like status, but also its sheer utility—as in you can use it a lot more ways than just as a slice on a plate. So we'll start with some basics, and then roll into making one that can be turned into a jillion things:

"JUST BECAUSE IT'S CALLED A LOAF DOESN'T MEAN YOU NEED A 'LOAF' PAN—I NEVER USE ONE."

THE BASICS FOR A 2-POUNDER

- **Meat:** 2 pounds of ground something like beef, pork, veal, chicken, turkey, or even a combo mix (half ground beef & half ground pork is very good), but no fish—a "fishloaf" just sounds disgusting.

- **Crumbs:** ¾ cup regular bread crumbs, whole wheat, panko, or even busted-up crackers

- **Liquid:** about ⅓ cup milk, broth, beer, whatever

- **Seasoning:** salt, pepper, and anything else that works for you

- **Eggs:** 2 large, beaten

- **Glaze for the top:** About a cup or so of something—ketchup, BBQ sauce, steak sauce, chili sauce, Asian hoisin—it's up to you. With all that, you could make a very respectable meatloaf. Now comes time for the add-ins—stuff to perk it up.

- **Diced and cooked veggies:** A mixture of carrot, celery, and bell peppers or spinach cooked with chopped garlic is amazing.

- **Cut-up bacon:** of course

- **Cheese:** A big handful of grated Parmesan or even feta cheese is great on top or even thrown into a middle layer.

- **Herbs:** fresh or dried

- **Spaghetti sauce**

OKAY! THAT'S ALL REALLY GREAT, BUT LET'S MAKE ONE ALREADY . . .

SAM'S MEXICAN MEATLOAF

The work involved here is nothing more than a little mixing.

Makes one big 2-pound loaf

Loaf
- 2 pounds ground beef
- ¾ cup bread crumbs (Japanese panko crumbs work really well)
- 1 1-ounce packet store-bought fajita seasoning
- 4 ounces canned diced green chiles
- 2 large eggs, beaten

Glaze
- 1 cup ketchup
- ¼ cup apricot jam
- 2 teaspoons chopped canned chipotle peppers

Preheat the oven to 350°F.

Combine loaf ingredients, and either pack into a greased loaf pan or shape into a loaf on a greased baking sheet.

Mix the glaze ingredients together in a bowl and spread about half of the glaze over the meatloaf.

Bake the meatloaf for about an hour or until no longer pink inside.

Allow to cool slightly, slice into 1-inch-thick pieces, and glaze with the extra sauce before serving.

BTW

I think the best way to reheat meatloaf is by covering slices with plastic wrap and putting them in the microwave. The oven takes a long time and dries them out—this way helps keeps them really moist.

But the really amazing thing about meatloaf is how many incarnations it can have. Allow me to make my point using a simple **Q & A**—with me handling both parts, of course:

Q: When you make spaghetti sauce with meat, what do you use?

A: You often use ground beef.

Q: Correct. And what do you do with the ground beef?

A: You brown it first, add seasonings and then some kind of sauce.

Q: Right again. So if you took a piece of cooked meatloaf, crumbled it in a pan, and added some sauce, etc.—what would you have?

A: You'd have spaghetti sauce with much less work.

Q: Hey, wait! Was that a trick?

A: Not exactly, but do you see where I'm going here? I'm trying to get you not to look at meatloaf always like just a meatloaf. Look at it like a set of potential ingredients. Dig? You will.

THE AMAZING MEATLOAF SANDWICH

I don't think I need to be exact here. Just a few tips will open your eyes to what is maybe the best reason of all to make a meatloaf.

- Whatever bread you use, you should toast it.

- Make the meatloaf slices thick—don't stinge out.

- Don't use cold meatloaf—it should be medium hot.

- Add Chipotle Mayo (page 47)—it's amazing. Or serving it with some jarred pasta sauce you have in your pantry would be okay too.

THE AMAZING MEATLOAF SANDWICH

MEATLOAF SPAGHETTI SAUCE

Make about 3 cups

2 fat slices meatloaf, each about
1½ inches thick
1 cup Roasted Red Pepper Sauce
(page 42)

Place the meatloaf in a nonstick pan over medium heat. With the back of a spoon, crumble the meatloaf well.

Add the Roasted Red Pepper Sauce, mix well, and heat through.

Serve on something . . . check out the frozen pasta suggestion on page 170?

MEATLOAF SLOPPY JOES

Who doesn't like a sloppy? And with these, the messy work has already been done.

Serves 4

4   1-inch-thick slices meatloaf
⅓   cup BBQ sauce
1   15-ounce can tomato sauce
1   tablespoon Worcestershire sauce
4   hamburger buns, lightly toasted

Put the meatloaf slices in a skillet over medium heat and crumble them well using the back of a spoon.

Once the meatloaf is broken up, add the BBQ sauce, tomato sauce, and Worcestershire—mix well and heat through.

Serve on lightly toasted buns.

POTATOES 101

What a topic! I mean, this could take up the pages of an entire book. But my goal is merely to point out a few easy ways I like to prepare and eat potatoes.

THE DAY THAT WE SHOT THE MASHED POTATO TACOS FOR A SHOW—THE CREW (ALL 2 OF THEM) ATE ABOUT A DOZEN TACOS. THEY ARE THAT GOOD . . .

MASHED

Don't take this the wrong way, but I'm not giving you a recipe for mashed potatoes. They're just kind of a pain with all the washing, peeling, cutting, boiling, drying, mashing, adding the milk or cream, buttering, salt & peppering, lumps, no lumps, blah blah blah.

This book is about shortcuts, and buying them already done is one of my favorite shortcuts ever. If you're really into making them yourself, ask somebody's grandmother. But once you buy them, or make them, or steal them—whatever . . . here's what I do with them:

BLUE CHEESE MASHED POTATOES

I love adding things to mashed potatoes, and this version makes them very elegant with almost no work.

Makes about 2 cups

2 cups leftover mashed potatoes
¼ cup crumbled blue cheese
2 teaspoons olive oil

Put everything in a pot, stir to combine, and heat until nicely warmed through.

Serve.

MASHED POTATO TACOS

MASHED POTATO TACOS

Here's why you want extra mashed potatoes. This is another dopey-sounding recipe, but it's not. Well, it is dopey-sounding, but it's really good.

Makes 4

1½ cups leftover mashed
    potatoes
4 corn tortillas
2 tablespoons sour cream
4 teaspoons hot sauce
½ cup finely chopped green
    onions (scallions)
4 handfuls of potato
    chips—preferably the
    extra-crispy kettle kind

Warm the potatoes in a small pot or in the microwave until they are heated through.

Heat the tortillas in a nonstick skillet until they begin to get a little color in spots and a little crispy.

Spread some sour cream onto each tortilla. Add about ¼ of the mashed potato to each tortilla.

Drizzle with the hot sauce and then sprinkle with the green onions. Take a handful of potato chips and crush them on top of each taco.

Fold in half and serve.

BAKED

I realize a recipe for a baked potato may seem a little basic—but I have it here for two reasons. The first is that I get asked how to make one quite often. And second is that I hope by putting the recipe here, it'll remind people how great a simple baked potato is. Because they are really great, especially combined with the toppings that follow.

1 large potato—either russet or Idaho
Oil

Preheat the oven to 400°F.

Wash and scrub the potato well—no soap please, just water. Poke the potato all around with the tines of a fork. Coat lightly with the oil.

Place in the oven and bake for about an hour, or until tender—turn over halfway.

You can certainly microwave a potato, but then you won't get that crispy, oh-so-desirable outside. So don't.

I DON'T NEED TO DESCRIBE HOW TO EAT A BAKED POTATO, SO I'LL JUST SUGGEST A FEW ALTERNATE TOPPINGS:

Some diced-up steak and a little hit of steak sauce
Leftover roasted veggies
Salsa (my favorite)
Olive oil and some feta cheese
Cooked mushrooms
Hot sauce, leftover chicken, and a little ranch dressing
Caramelized red onions—lots of them
Chili
Crunchy Asian noodles and some teriyaki sauce

Look, I'm sure you already know what you're doing here, and I'm not trying to get up in your grill about what you eat, but think about this: A medium baked potato averages about 175 calories. The classic combination of butter, sour cream, bacon, and cheese you might top it with could easily add another 300 to 400 calories. Adding about a quarter cup of salsa instead would add only 20 calories. Just think about it.

SHEPHERD'S PIE

This is a great comfort food. Perfect for those cooler evenings or even warmer mornings—whenever.

Serves 8

1 teaspoon oil
1 small onion, diced
1 10-ounce package frozen baby peas
1 pound cooked roast beef, diced small (If I don't have any, I just buy a thick slice from the supermarket deli counter.)
6 ounces beef gravy
2 cups leftover mashed potatoes
Kosher salt and freshly ground pepper

Preheat the oven to 400°F.

Heat a large skillet over medium heat. Add the oil and onion and cook, stirring. When the onion is softened, stir in the peas.

Transfer the onion and peas to a large bowl. Stir in the beef and gravy.

Season the mashed potatoes with salt and pepper.

Place the beef mixture in the bottom of a 9 x 9–inch casserole dish and top evenly with the potatoes.

Place in the oven and bake for about 30 minutes, or until the top begins to get a little brown. Serve.

QUICK PIEROGIES

No fuss and no pierogi muss. These are so good you'll think a bunch of grandmas had a pierogi-making session in the basement of Mrs. Kowalczyk's house.

Makes about 18

1 cup leftover mashed potatoes
2 tablespoons grated cheddar cheese
½ teaspoon kosher salt
18 round won ton wrappers
Butter
Sour cream and hot sauce (optional), for serving

Bring a pot of water to a boil. In a bowl, combine the potatoes, cheese, and salt and mix well.

Put about a tablespoon of the potato mixture in the middle of each wrapper. Dip your finger in a little water and lightly wet the edge all the way around. Fold over (trying to push out any air pockets) and seal the edge.

Boil for about 2 minutes, or until they float.

Heat a little butter in a nonstick skillet, remove the pierogi from the boiling water, shake dry, and panfry until light brown and a little crispy.

Serve with sour cream (and if I was eating them, also with a little hot sauce).

"A QUIET, CONTEMPLATIVE MOMENT WHILE SHOOTING PICTURES FOR THE BOOK. OR MAYBE IT WAS JUST A THIRSTY MOMENT. WHATEVER."

getting ready to shoot the meatloaf

ROASTED

Simple roasted potatoes are a really nice thing, and they smell amazing while cooking. In a pinch, you can dice them, oil them, throw them on a pan, and stick them in the oven. And you can do this with pretty much any type of potato.

GARLIC ROASTED POTATOES

About as simple as it gets. I like to double the recipe so I have extra for some kind of breakfast thing the next morning.

Makes 4 servings

- 2 pounds new potatoes, washed and dried
- 1 head garlic, cloves separated and peeled
- ¼ cup olive oil
  Kosher salt
  Freshly ground black pepper

Preheat the oven to 425°F.

Cut the potatoes into quarters and put in a large bowl with the garlic and olive oil. Season with salt and mix well to coat.

Spread on a baking sheet and bake for about an hour—give them a shake at the halfway point.

Transfer to a serving bowl and season with freshly ground pepper.

Herb Roasted Potatoes:

Same as above, but swap about 3 tablespoons chopped fresh thyme or rosemary for the garlic—they'll be so good you'll go crazy.

Sour Cream & Caviar Roasted Potatoes:

This is a dinner version of breakfast potatoes I like to eat. Same as the Garlic Roasted, but with no garlic. When you plate them, add a big spoonful of sour cream to the top and a little (not expensive) caviar to the top of that. Sprinkle some chopped green onions and freshly ground pepper over all of it.

MORE THOUGHTS ON LEFTOVERS

I want to encourage you NOT to look at leftover anything the same way again—especially meat & potatoes. I also realize you might need a little inspiration, so here goes.

Do This: Once a week you should make something only out of what's in your fridge. Don't use anything new; don't open anything—just use straight leftovers. And if you do, two things will happen. The first, obviously, is that you'll save money instead of throwing it away. And second, you might actually make something really good.

And in case you need more inspiration, here are a few leftover ideas. Get it? "Leftover ideas"?

- Leftover roast beef becomes Shepherd's Pie (page 158).

- Leftover chicken becomes Chicken & Bacon Pot Pie (page 124).

- Leftover anything can become a quesadilla—you know that, right? You just need some cheese to keep the thing together because it works like glue.

- Leftovers can become tacos—same principal as quesadillas, though the cheese part is not really important.

- French fries from last night become a Breakfast Burrito (page 208).

- Cooked sausages from a brunch thing can be crumbled into corn-meal muffins or added to pancakes.

- Leftover mashed potatoes can be mixed with diced bacon, etc. and rolled in bread crumbs to make potato pancake things.

No self-respecting cookbook dealing with shortcuts would be complete without some discussion about pasta, arguably one of the quickest and easiest things to make. The key is simple—keep a few boxes of this inexpensive item around and use them. But go for different shapes and sizes; you'll be glad you did. Boxed pasta is less than 10 minutes in the water once it boils—you can handle that amount of time, right? And if you can't, then the frozen pasta will be right up your alley.

PASTA

- here's a cool pasta thing . . . it can be frozen—who knew?

- whipping cream—the basic starter sauce

- pink sauce

- a darn simple red clam sauce

- blue cheese gnocchi with bacon

- quick pasta sauces

- roasted tomato pasta

- simple pasta with garlic

- pasta with smoked salmon

HERE'S A COOL PASTA THING . . . IT CAN BE FROZEN—WHO KNEW?

In the interest of cooking quickly, you can precook a bunch of pasta and freeze it in smaller portions, like in zipper-top plastic bags. Then, it's really as simple as opening a bag, running warm water over it in a colander in the sink, and tossing it with whatever you want in a pan to finish. But before you get all holier-than-thou on me, I'm suggesting you remember three things:

- This is a book on shortcuts that you willingly purchased.

- I care about you.

- This is a book on shortcuts.

HOW TO FREEZE & USE FROZEN PASTA

Pretty much any kind of pasta works, but I find it's easier to deal with short pasta, like penne, rigatoni, or a macaroni.

Add pasta to a pot of boiling water, but cook for about a minute less than what the package says.

Rinse the pasta with cool water to stop the cooking and drain really well. Really well.

Put in zipper-top plastic bags—the sandwich-size bags I send my rats off to school with is about the perfect amount for one person—and freeze.

Remove the bag from the freezer, open it, and fill it with hot water for about a minute.

Drain and do whatever you want to sauce it.

But they don't last forever.

Try to use them within 3 to 4 weeks.

WHIPPING CREAM— THE BASIC STARTER SAUCE

With nothing more than a little un-whipped heavy whipping cream, you can make something pretty amazing. My general rule of thumb is to use about ½ cup whipping cream for every 2 cups of cooked pasta.

Put the cream in a small pot or nonstick pan over medium heat and start to simmer. Add about 1 tablespoon shredded Parmesan and allow to thicken. Add the pasta and stir until everything is heated. Season well with kosher salt and freshly ground pepper and you've got the world's fastest Alfredo sauce.

PINK SAUCE

Perfect for any pasta, shrimp, or scallop thing, or even a piece of seared fish you might have. Add a little chopped fresh basil and you'll be very happy.

Makes about 2½ cups

2 cups pasta sauce, any kind—you know I mean the store-bought version, right?

½ cup heavy whipping cream

Heat the pasta sauce and whipping cream in a nonstick pan. Let simmer about 5 minutes and add to anything.

A DARN SIMPLE RED CLAM SAUCE

My friend Danielle turned me on to this when our sons played soccer together. Don't get all weirded out by the V8—it's really good.

Makes about 3 cups

- 2 tablespoons butter
- 2 tablespoons finely chopped garlic
- 2 tablespoons flour
- 2 5.5-ounce cans regular V8™ juice
- 2 6.5-ounce cans chopped clams
- 2 tablespoons chopped fresh basil
  Cooked linguine or spaghetti, for serving

Heat a nonstick pan over medium heat. Melt the butter, then add the garlic. Cook the garlic for a minute, then stir in the flour. Slowly stir in the V8 and the juice from the clams—simmer for about 10 minutes.

Add the clams and basil and heat through.

Serve over linguine or spaghetti.

QUICK PASTA SAUCES

1. SOUR CREAM & CHILI

This may be another weird-sounding thing—until you do it.

For every 2 cups of cooked pasta, use about ⅓ cup sour cream, ¼ cup chili sauce (the non-Asian kind), ¼ teaspoon chili flakes, salt and pepper, and a sprinkle of chopped parsley.

Put cooked pasta in a small pot and add the sour cream and chili sauce.

Stir until everything is heated.

Season with salt and pepper and add a little chopped parsley.

2. PESTO

Once again, pesto saves the day. I add about ¼ cup pesto, a tablespoon of olive oil, and a teaspoon of red pepper flakes for every 2 cups of cooked pasta.

Put the cooked pasta in a small pot and add the pesto, olive oil, and red pepper flakes. Stir until everything is heated.

Season with freshly ground black pepper and serve.

3. PEANUT BUTTER
I am so not kidding.

For a quick Asian flavor, combine ⅓ cup peanut butter (crunchy is great), 2 tablespoons soy sauce, ½ cup chicken broth, and just short of a teaspoon Asian chili sauce. Mix it all in a little pot until thick and warm, then add 2 cups pasta and mix well. Add a little chopped cilantro if you have it. For a bigger deal, I like to serve this pasta with some grilled chicken.

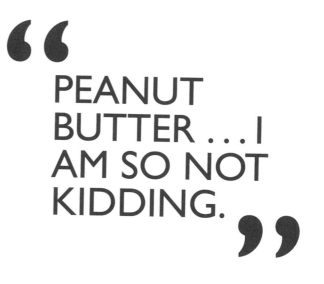

"PEANUT BUTTER ... I AM SO NOT KIDDING. "

BLUE CHEESE GNOCCHI WITH BACON

I love blue cheese, and I love gnocchi—those little potato pasta deals. They're shelf-stable and can hang for almost ever. But since this is a little rich, I'd go with it as a side dish or an appetizer instead of the main event.

Serves 6

- 8 ounces half-and-half
- 3 ounces blue cheese crumbles
- I pound gnocchi
- I ounce "ready" bacon, cooked and crumbled
- Kosher salt and freshly ground black pepper

Bring a large pot of water to a boil.

Put the half-and-half and blue cheese in a small pot over medium heat. Stir well—you want the blue cheese melted into the cream.

Add the gnocchi to the boiling water.

When the gnocchi float (about 3 minutes), drain and add to the cream sauce—mix well and transfer to a plate or bowl.

Crumble the bacon on top and season with salt and pepper.

BLUE CHEESE GNOCCHI WITH BACON

ROASTED TOMATO PASTA

ROASTED TOMATO PASTA

This is a totally fresh, not heavily sauced pasta. You'll love the roasted tomatoes so much, you'll be lucky if they all make it onto the pasta.

Serves 6

- 2 pounds small tomatoes (cherry tomatoes)
- 3 cloves garlic, chopped fine
- 3 tablespoons olive oil
  Kosher salt and freshly ground black pepper
- 1 pound pasta
- ¼ cup shredded Parmesan cheese
  Chopped parsley or basil, for garnish

Preheat the oven to 425°F and put a large pot of water on the stove to boil.

Cut the tomatoes in half and place in a medium bowl with the garlic, half the oil, and salt and pepper to taste. Mix well. Put the tomatoes on a baking sheet in a single layer.

Bake about 20 minutes, or until they get all soft, squishy, and beautiful. During the tomatoes' last 10 minutes in the oven, cook the pasta according to the package directions—drain well.

Combine the pasta, tomatoes, remaining oil, and Parmesan cheese in a bowl and toss.

Garnish and serve.

"WE FEED HALEY & LUCKY DOG FOOD, & DO EVERYTHING IN OUR POWER NOT TO GIVE THEM PEOPLE FOOD. BUT LOOK AT THEM—IT'S SO HARD TO SAY NO SOMETIMES . . ."

they had a busy day.

SIMPLE PASTA WITH GARLIC

So simple—yet totally great. You have to like garlic for this one, though.

Serves 6

1 pound pasta—spaghetti is good here
¼ cup olive oil
4 big cloves garlic, sliced thin
Chopped fresh parsley
Shredded Parmesan cheese
Freshly ground black pepper

Cook the pasta according to the package directions.

Heat the olive oil in a small pan over medium-low heat. Add the sliced garlic and lightly brown it in the oil for maybe 2 minutes. (Do not over brown or it becomes bitter.)

Drain the cooked pasta and put back in the pot. Add the olive oil with garlic, some chopped fresh parsley, and Parmesan. Mix well.

To serve, plate with a bit more Parmesan cheese. Season with black pepper to taste.

PASTA WITH SMOKED SALMON

I've already told you to keep pasta and heavy whipping cream around. So all you need now is the smoked salmon and peas, and you're golden.

Serves 6

1 pound penne pasta
1 tablespoon butter
½ pound thinly sliced smoked salmon, chopped up
1 cup frozen peas, no need to defrost them
1 cup heavy whipping cream
Kosher salt and freshly ground black pepper

Bring a large pot of water to a boil and cook the pasta according to the package directions.

Melt the butter in a nonstick pan over medium heat and add the salmon and peas. Cook until heated through, about 2 minutes.

Add the cream and season with salt and pepper to taste. Stir well and keep at a low simmer—allow to thicken slightly.

Drain the pasta and toss with the salmon and pea mixture. Serve.

If I can keep something in my freezer that makes my food life easier, I will. And I don't care what the food snobs think. The following things can work wonders if you have them on hand. Allow me to elaborate:

YOUR BFF —YOUR BEST FROZEN FRIEND

- frozen shrimp • cheater seafood paella

- shrimp BLT • shrimp foo-yung

- barbequed shrimp • pie dough

- pot pie or stew lids • turnovers

- frozen french fries • poutine

- fries with grazy • BTW

- breakfast burrito

- aunt Toby's hash brown casserole

- frozen meatballs

- meatball philly cheese steak

- meatball stroganoff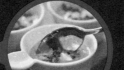

- frozen vegetables • frozen diced onions

- mushroom-onion burgers • frozen peas

- pea soup • tuna casserole

- frozen spinach • creamed spinach with bacon

- spinach & goat cheese omelet

- spinach dip-filled sourdough loaf

- fish sticks • fish tacos • fish burritos

- frozen pot stickers • frozen fruit

- zamba • frozen margarita

FROZEN SHRIMP

I mentioned the importance of frozen raw shrimp in my first book, and I'll do it again here. They defrost really easy, and can go from zip to amazing in only a few minutes. Remember, they're measured by how many there are in a pound. I normally buy 31/40s. But for the BLT that follows, go bigger, like 21/25s.

Here are a few ideas:

- **Grilled Shrimp Salad:** Toss a big handful of shrimp with the same dressing you'll use for your salad and then either put them on the grill or quickly cook them in a nonstick pan. I'd go with an oil-based kind of dressing. Tossing stuff in something thick and then grilling is kind of nasty.

- **Simple Surf and Turf:** Throw a couple skewers of shrimp on the grill when you take the meat off to rest. When the shrimp is ready, the meat will be, too.

- **On a Pizza:** With pretty much anything else.

- **In a Soup:** Grab a can of potato soup, get it simmering, add raw, peeled shrimp in the last 5 minutes of cooking, and presto chango— you've suddenly got potato and shrimp chowder (don't forget to add a little chopped parsley).

CHEATER SEAFOOD PAELLA

Considering this is based on a packaged rice mix—it's amazing (with almost none of the work to make regular paella). If you can make and serve this in a big sauté pan, it'll look way more legit. If you can't— no big deal.

Serves 8

2 7-ounce packages Rice-a-Roni ® "Spanish" Rice
¾ pound raw shrimp, peeled and deveined
1 pound fresh mussels
1 lemon, cut into 8 wedges

Cook the rice according to the package directions, but add the shrimp and mussels (and re-cover) for the last 7 minutes of cooking.

Remove the lid, stand back, and marvel at your excellence.

Serve with a big fat wedge of lemon on the side.

Be sure to discard any mussels that haven't opened (because they were DOA and can make you very sick).

CHEATER SEAFOOD PAELLA

SHRIMP BLT

This is a nice change from the everyday BLT (which is still right near the top of the sandwich world), but change is good all the same. For a real change, cook the shrimp on your BBQ . . .

Makes 2 large sandwiches

¾ pound large peeled raw shrimp—21/25s are good here

1 teaspoon oil

Kosher salt and freshly ground black pepper to taste

2 nice sandwich rolls (hoagie style)

Chili sauce, the ketchup-y kind, not the Asian kind

About 8 pieces "ready" bacon, cooked and crispy

1 cup shredded iceberg lettuce

1 medium-sized ripe tomato, sliced

Preheat a pan over medium heat, toss in the shrimp and oil, and season to taste with salt and pepper. Cook, stirring, until pink. (These will cook quickly.)

Meanwhile, toast the rolls lightly—either in a toaster or under the broiler.

Spread the chili sauce to taste on the rolls, then add bacon, lettuce, and tomato slices to each.

Add the cooked shrimp and the other roll half.

SHRIMP FOO-YUNG

I know to some of you this won't sound all that good . . . a big Chinese shrimp omelet with bean sprouts and gravy. Actually, now that I've written that, it does sound kind of creepy, doesn't it? But you must believe. It had been years since I'd eaten any kind of foo-yung, and even then it was in a restaurant, not at home. But now that I've rediscovered it, I'm a happy foo-yung-eatin' guy.

Serves 4

8 ounces chicken gravy
2 tablespoons soy sauce
6 large eggs
1 cup fresh bean sprouts
1 cup peeled and cooked bay shrimp, those little tiny guys that you never know what to do with
⅓ cup finely chopped green onions (scallions), white and light green parts only
½ tablespoon oil

Put the gravy and soy sauce into a small pot, stir well, and set over low heat.

Preheat about a 9-inch nonstick skillet over medium heat.

Crack the eggs into a bowl and beat with a fork. Add the sprouts, shrimp, and green onions (saving a little for garnish) and mix well.

Add the oil to the skillet and pour in the egg mixture. Cook for 2 to 3 minutes, or until the bottom is set, then flip to cook the other side.

Once both sides are cooked, remove from the pan, cut into wedges, put on a plate, and spoon some gravy over.

BARBEQUED SHRIMP

BARBEQUED SHRIMP

At the absolute last minute you can have an awesome, delicious, and fun meal. But it's a shame to eat these puppies alone—turn them into a party. Oh, and puppy is merely a euphemism—I would never eat a real puppy, honest.

Serves 4 to 6 as a meal, and maybe 10 as an appetizer

1 stick butter
2 tablespoons chopped fresh garlic
2 pounds raw shrimp (31/40s) or larger, shells on
1 tablespoon Old Bay seasoning
1 12-ounce bottle darkish beer
1 tablespoon Worcestershire sauce
Juice of 1 lemon
Crusty bread, for serving

Melt half the butter with the garlic in a large pan over medium heat. Add the shrimp and Old Bay and cook, stirring, until the shrimp are pink.

Add the remaining butter, the beer, Worcestershire, and lemon juice and heat through.

Serve in bowls so you can dip the warm crusty bread.

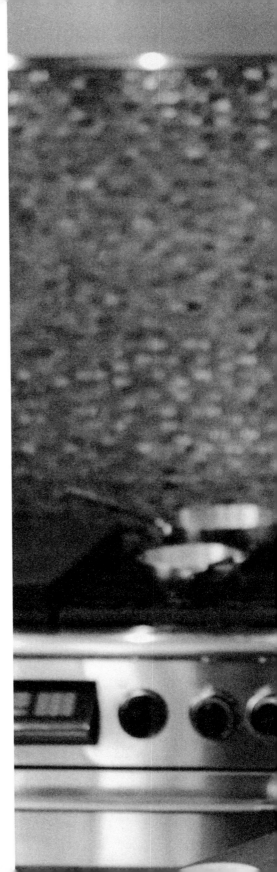

PIE DOUGH

As far as I'm concerned, anything wrapped in pie dough is amazing. Old shoes, milk cartons—I don't care. If it's got beautifully cooked dough near it—I'm going to eat it.

"AS FAR AS I'M CONCERNED ANYTHING WRAPPED IN PIE DOUGH IS AMAZING. OLD SHOES, MILK CARTONS—I DON'T CARE. IF IT'S GOT BEAUTIFULLY COOKED DOUGH NEAR IT—I'M GOING TO EAT IT. "

POT PIE OR STEW LIDS

Put some kind of canned stew, chili, or even soup in an ovenproof bowl, and cover with a circle of uncooked pie dough. Bake at 350°F until the crust has browned and serve.

TURNOVERS

Cut out 4-inch circles of dough and put a table-spoon or two of some kind of filling in the middle. You can use sweet things like jam, canned pie filling, mashed sweet potato, etc. Or go the other way and put in vegetables, meat, poultry, even stuffing—weird maybe, but I like it. Brush the edges with a little beaten egg, then fold over and seal the edges together. Brush the top with a little egg and then sprinkle the sweet ones with a little sugar, or the not-sweet ones with something like sesame seeds, coarse salt, or cracked black pepper. Bake at 350°F until nicely browned, 20 to 25 minutes.

FROZEN FRENCH FRIES

Good as is, in a burrito, or in the Manedict (page 78). And as in any of the following . . . yummm.

the manedict with fries

POUTINE

If there was ever a food that might be considered "Canadian," this would likely be it.

Serves 4

1 26-ounce bag frozen French fries, the thin straight kind—not those crazy curly ones
1 12-ounce jar chicken gravy
1 teaspoon Worcestershire sauce
1 teaspoon freshly ground black pepper
1 cup cheese curds, if you can find them—if not, use shredded mozzarella

Cook the fries according to the package instructions—get them brown and crispy.

While the fries cook, mix the gravy with the Worcestershire sauce and some pepper to taste in a small pot. Heat over low until hot.

Break up the cheese curds (or open the bag of mozzarella). In four bowls, layer as follows: French fries, cheese, gravy. Add a little more freshly ground black pepper to taste.

Be sure to get a little of everything in each bite. Now go watch a little hockey, ya hoser.

FRIES WITH GRAVY

The simple version of Poutine, of course, is simply fries with gravy—and if you keep fries in the freezer and gravy in the pantry (like I told you to do), you'll be able to make this almost anytime you want. I really want to encourage you to try the Poutine (see preceding recipe), but this is still stupidly amazing. I can hear my editor, Justin, saying something like "Really? And I suppose your next recipe will be for a glass of water." I don't care, because this is the time-honored way of eating fries where I grew up. It doesn't really even need a recipe—you should be able to get it from the title. But because I'd never want to take anyone's cooking instincts for granted, here goes:

Serves however many

Cooked French fries
Gravy, warmed

Pour the gravy over the fries.
Eat.

TW

If I'm ever having a French-fry emergency and need them like now, here's what I do:

Preheat the broiler.

Take as many fries as I need and spread them out on a plate.

Microwave the plate for about 1 minute, or until the fries are all soft.

Put the fries on a baking sheet and put under the broiler—about 3 inches away from the heat.

Broil until crisp, but be sure to mix often to prevent burning. So instead of waiting 15 minutes for the oven to heat and then another 15 for the fries to bake, mine are done in less than 10. Now that's a shortcut . . .

" . . . YOU'LL BE ABLE TO MAKE THIS ALMOST ANY-TIME YOU WANT. "

"I REMEMBER THIS SHOT, AND MY MOUTH WAS COMPLETELY JAMMED WITH FOOD. I DON'T MIND PICTURES, BUT NOT LIKE THIS. AND LOOK, THERE'S EVEN FOOD ON MY FINGERS . . ."

no pictures while I'm eating

BREAKFAST BURRITO

My oldest Max would eat one of these every time he went to the local taco shop. So I of course had to start making them, and eventually found the key . . . frozen French fries. It was either pure genius or pure laziness—one of the two.

Makes 4

1 teaspoon oil
½ cup diced onion (red, white, or yellow)
2 big handfuls frozen French fries
  About a cup of any combination of the following: any kind of cooked meat—ham, steak, pastrami, meatloaf—yes, even meatloaf; leftover grilled veggies
4 large eggs
  Kosher salt and freshly ground black pepper
4 tortillas or wraps, burrito size
¼ cup sour cream
⅓ cup shredded cheese, any kind
  Hot sauce

Heat the oil in a nonstick pan. Add the onion and cook, stirring, until softened.

Spread the fries out on a plate, microwave for about a minute, then dice and immediately add to the onion.

Add any precooked item(s)—meat or veggies—and continue to cook until everything is well mixed and heated through.

Beat the eggs (with some salt and pepper) and add to the pan mixture. Stir well to combine.
While all this cooks, heat the tortillas in a skillet or the microwave.

Take a tortilla and spread it with about 1 tablespoon of the sour cream and add about ¼ of the filling. Sprinkle with cheese, add a few dashes of hot sauce, and roll it up burrito style.

AUNT TOBY'S HASH BROWN CASSEROLE,
AKA MUSHROOM SOUP THING FOR KELLY

Apart from eating mushroom soup, I've only used it for tuna casserole. But for years now my mother has told me about this legendary, in fact almost cult-like side dish that was presumably started by my Aunt Toby. I'm not saying it wasn't invented by her; I just don't want a Babs Finkelstein or someone suing me because she was really the inventor. Every Jewish home in Vancouver has made it at some point or another over the past forty years I think. It's a delightful mélange of hash browns, mushroom soup, and cheddar cheese (if that combination of ingredients can be called a mélange).

So, I call my mom to get the recipe and surprise, surprise, Aunt Toby is there visiting. What follows is the recipe I got while on the phone with her… which took about forty-five minutes. Apparently after forty years, people make a recipe their own—and there was a great deal of disagreement. They argued about a lot of it—heat, how long, the type of cheese, and whether breadcrumbs belonged on top or not. Take it for what it is. I think in the Midwest they'd call this a "hot dish."

Serves about 20 Vancouver Jews, as a side dish

2 tablespoons butter, melted
1 pound frozen cubed hash browns—Toby says not the shredded kind
2 bunches green onions (scallions), chopped
2 cans cream of mushroom soup, for Kelly
2 cups grated cheddar cheese (Toby says nothing generic—go for a name brand here)
2 cups sour cream
   Pinch of salt

Preheat the oven to 350°F.

Melt the butter and mix it with the remaining ingredients.

Put everything in a 3-quart baking dish (that's my mom's advice).

Bake for 1 hour, if you listen to Aunt Toby—or 1 hour and 15 minutes, if you listen to my mom. Serve.

FROZEN MEATBALLS

You do know that you can simply take frozen meatballs and put them directly into a pot with jarred pasta sauce over medium/low heat and about 20 minutes later they'll be hot, moist, and ready to eat. You know that, right?

Well, now you do—and that's why I like them. But I also like them for these things:

MEATBALL PHILLY CHEESE STEAK

I've never been to Philly, I don't know anyone from Philly, and even if I did I'm sure they'd want to slug me for using meatballs instead of steak. But you know what? I don't worry about that because this is awesome without their advice. Just make it and enjoy it.

Probably makes 4

1 tablespoon oil
1 yellow onion, thinly sliced
1 green pepper, thinly sliced
20 frozen meatballs (the little guys work here), defrosted
2 tablespoons Worcestershire sauce
4 fresh sandwich rolls, split in half crosswise and lightly toasted
4 slices provolone cheese
Kosher salt and freshly ground black pepper

Heat a nonstick skillet over medium heat. Add the oil, then the onion and pepper and cook until softened.

Mix in the meatballs and Worcestershire and heat through.

Put some of the meatball-onion-pepper mixture on each toasted bun, add the cheese, and melt under the broiler. Season with salt and pepper.

MEATBALL STROGANOFF

This uses two of my favorite supermarket ingredients—frozen meatballs and jarred gravy. It's like the planets are in total meatball alignment.

Serves 6

1 teaspoon oil
½ cup diced onion
1 pound frozen meatballs (I like the little guys), defrosted
1 12-ounce jar beef gravy
1 cup sour cream
2 tablespoons prepared horseradish (not the creamed kind)
3 tablespoons chopped fresh dill—or 1 tablespoon dried
Wide egg noodles, for serving

Heat the oil in a large skillet. Add the onion and cook, stirring, until softened.

Add the defrosted meatballs to the same pan. Add the gravy, sour cream, horseradish, and dill and stir until mixed well. Heat through.

Serve over noodles—preferably those big, wide egg noodles. Garnish with a little freshly chopped dill, if you have it.

MEATBALL STROGANOFF

FROZEN VEGETABLES

In general, frozen vegetables are not just easier to deal with than fresh, they're just as good because they're picked when they're at maximum flavor, then sorted, separated, cleaned, portioned out, and quickly frozen. So by the time you get them, it's like someone's grandma in a frilly apron has spent a few hours lovingly caring for them. Look, if you're making Sunday dinner, have the time, and have a choice between frozen green beans and fresh—the fresh should win. But at 7:30 on a Wednesday when you're dying for a quick stir-fry using the black bean sauce from your shortcut pantry . . . you'll be really happy the frozen beans are there. And the best part is you don't need to thaw frozen vegetables first. Use as little water as possible, and cook just until the vegetables are done the way you like— and I'm really hoping that doesn't mean mushy. The point is—don't diss them, appreciate them for what they are and what they can do for you. Like this:

FROZEN DICED ONIONS

I discovered these recently and they are, in a word, "genius." But because onions are one of the most labor-intensive veggies out there, they're often missed, which is sad really. But it doesn't have to be like that. A bag of already diced and frozen onions will not just go in a jillion things, they'll also cook in record time.

Try them in any of this junk:

- Anything that has eggs in it.

- Name a taco—and these will add to the flavor without adding to the work.

- Mix in a handful when you're making burgers and your burger will just be . . . better. Or if you buy premade burgers, simply cook a bunch of them with presliced mushrooms for something great to put on top—like this:

MUSHROOM-ONION BURGERS

So simple. So amazing.

Makes 6

 1 teaspoon oil
 2 cups frozen diced onions
16 ounces sliced mushrooms
    Kosher salt and freshly ground
    black pepper
 2 tablespoons soy sauce
 6 burgers—go on, you decide
    what kind
 6 slices cheese (this is a good
    time to give creamy havarti a
    chance)
 6 buns (if you could get creative
    here I'd love you forever, see
    Note 2)

Heat the oil in a nonstick pan over medium heat. Add the onions and mushrooms and cook, stirring, until softened. Season with salt and pepper, then stir in the soy sauce—set aside.

Meanwhile, prepare the burgers. Add cheese to the second side when you flip them and cook until done.

Throw 'em on a bun and add a bunch of the onion/mushroom mix.

BTW—The obvious shortcut with these burgers would be to sub the fresh mushrooms with canned.

Don't—canned mushrooms are creepy, I was just testing you.

BTW2—"Be creative with the bun" means using a focaccia roll or a bagel or an onion roll, that would be sweet—but not like "sweet" sweet—like "cool" sweet—or a really good toasted rye bread (as in a diner "patty melt").

FROZEN PEAS

Great in anything with rice—like fried rice. Just throw a handful in the pan or wok at the beginning, and they'll be ready by the time the rice is done. Pasta—dump some in the boiling water a couple of minutes before the pasta is done. Then drain the whole deal and carry on. And hey, they're really good in this:

PEA SOUP

PEA SOUP

This is not that thick gross Army-green stuff. This is fresh-tasting, bright green (it's on the cover), and really delicious . . . and it starts in the freezer.

Makes 4 to 6 servings

2 teaspoons olive oil
½ cup diced red onion
1 2-ounce package "ready" bacon, diced small
3 cups chicken broth
1 16-ounce bag frozen peas
Kosher salt and freshly ground black pepper
¼ cup heavy whipping cream
Sour cream

Heat the oil in a nonstick pan over medium heat.

Add the onion and cook, stirring, until softened, then add the bacon and continue cooking until both are crispy—set aside.

In a medium pot, bring the broth to a boil and add the peas. Cook for about 2 minutes.

Transfer the peas in a blender with just enough of the broth to cover and season with salt and pepper.

Blend until smooth. Return to the pot and stir in the cream. Heat through. Serve in a bowl topped with a spoonful of sour cream and some of the onion/bacon mixture.

TUNA CASSEROLE

This is old-school food at its best—one bite and you'll be thinking of lava lamps, *The Dick Van Dyke Show*, and shag carpet. Taste it again for the first time.

Serves 8

1   16-ounce box shell pasta
1   12-ounce can tuna (I like chunk albacore in water), drained
2   cups grated cheddar cheese
1   8-ounce can cream of mushroom soup
1   10-ounce bag frozen peas
2   cups regular salted potato chips, crumbled

Preheat the oven to 375°F.

Cook the shells for 2 minutes less than directed by the package, then drain.

Mix the tuna, cheese, soup, and peas together in a large bowl. Add the pasta and mix well.

Transfer everything to a casserole dish and top with the crumbled chips.

Bake for 30 minutes and enjoy.

FROZEN SPINACH

I love this stuff and like to throw it in anything I can . . .

- Add a big-ass frozen handful to some jarred pasta sauce and let it simmer.

- Mix it into a meatloaf before baking.

- Stuff a chicken breast. Make a slit in the side of a chicken breast to make a pocket. Cook the spinach according to the package directions, add Parmesan and seasonings, and cram into the chicken breast—then grill.

- Creamed spinach—holy crap . . .

CREAMED SPINACH WITH BACON

Shhhhh, don't talk. Just cook a steak and throw some of this on the side. You can thank me later . . .

Serves 4

- 2 10-ounce boxes frozen chopped spinach, thawed
- 1 ounce "ready" bacon, chopped
  Kosher salt and freshly ground black pepper
- 1½ cups heavy whipping cream
- 4 tablespoons grated Parmesan cheese

Squeeze the spinach dry in a colander.

Put the bacon in a nonstick pan over medium heat and cook until it starts to get a wee bit crispy.

Add the spinach and salt and pepper to taste and cook, stirring, until the spinach is warmed through—then add cream and Parmesan.

Continue stirring until everything is nicely warmed, thicker, creamier, and totally bitchin'.

OR THIS FAV . . .

SPINACH & GOAT CHEESE OMELET

There's just something so right about this, it's crazy. And while an omelet with, say, bacon and mushrooms is excellent for breakfast, this version seems to cross all mealtime boundaries. It's not just good for breakfast, lunch, and dinner, but especially late night—as in just the two of you . . . a couple glasses of a crisp white wine . . . on the roof under a big blanket. See where I'm going with this?

Makes 1 omelet

A handful of thawed frozen spinach (I can hear my editor moaning about how people need exact amounts, so I'll be a little more clear: whatever fits exactly in your own hand should be fine.)
2 large eggs
Kosher salt and freshly ground pepper
Butter
2 to 3 tablespoons goat cheese crumbles

Heat a nonstick skillet over medium heat and add the frozen spinach. Cook until there's no more liquid (but not until it starts sticking).

In a small bowl, beat the eggs with a pinch of salt and pepper.

Add about a teaspoon of butter to the spinach and let it melt. Spread the spinach evenly over the pan. Pour the eggs over the spinach, mix gently, and cook, pulling the edges away from the pan with a spatula and letting the uncooked egg run underneath.

When the eggs are mostly set but still a tiny bit moist on top, add cheese crumbles on one half. Fold the other half over to cover the crumbles and let it cook for about a minute.

Flip the entire omelet over to the second side and cook for another minute or so until it's cooked to your "egg liking"—dry, not dry, it's up to you.

Give it a touch more fresh ground pepper, grab two forks and a blanket, and head up to the roof.

"I EAT HOT FOOD—OKAY, REALLY HOT FOOD SOMETIMES AND I'M OKAY WITH IT. IT MAY NOT BE THE SMARTEST THING, BUT THEN I'M NOT THE SMART-EST GUY—SO IT WORKS OUT."

so many pictures . . . i'm hiding!

SPINACH DIP–FILLED SOURDOUGH LOAF

Perhaps the most overdone take-to-a-party appetizer on the planet. You didn't really think I'd put a recipe in here for this, did you? Not only do I hate it, but I think it should be banned forever. In fact, anyone caught serving it should be forced to eat nothing but this for six months straight. That'll teach 'em.

Makes 1 loaf

FISH STICKS. NO, SERIOUSLY . . .

I am not suggesting you serve them "as is" with mashed potatoes for dinner. I'm suggesting you just think outside the cardboard fish-stick box they came in. Look, we love our Mexican food in Southern California and I remember biting into a fish taco one day at a little taco shop and thinking, "Holy crap, this is really good." Fish tacos are usually made with either a piece of deep-fried fish or a fresh grilled piece. But two bites later I realized this one was made with frozen fish sticks. Now before you throw away this book and threaten to rip my head off—don't you think you should try them first?

"JUST THINK OUTSIDE THE CARD-BOARD FISH-STICK BOX . . . "

FISH (STICK) TACOS

Crispy, crunchy, and at 1 A.M. after a long night and you're absolutely starving . . . you'll call me a genius. I mean, you'll call them genius.

Makes 6 tacos

12 fish sticks (the frozen kind that are about the size of a finger)
6 corn tortillas—if you don't like corn tortillas, learn to . . .
⅓ cup Salsa Cream (page 40)
½ cup shredded green cabbage
1 lime, cut into 6 wedges
Hot sauce, optional

Cook the fish sticks according to the package directions.
Warm the tortillas—a nonstick pan is ideal.
Put some Salsa Cream on each tortilla, then 2 sticks, some cabbage, a squeeze of the lime, and then a few shakes of the hot sauce.

I realize that until you've had one, a fish taco can sound pretty creepy, so the following fish burrito is potentially going to sound way worse. But you've gotta trust me, because if you don't, then the chance you'll try the Cap'n Crunch Seared Tuna on page 71 goes completely out the window.

FISH (STICK) BURRITOS

Makes 6 burritos

18 fish sticks, the frozen kind
6 flour tortillas, burrito size
1 cup canned refried beans
⅓ cup Salsa Cream (page 40)
1 cup Mexican rice, the packaged kind, cooked
1 lime, cut into wedges

Cook the fish sticks according to the package directions.

Warm the tortillas—a nonstick pan is ideal.

Put some of the refried beans in the middle of each tortilla, then the Salsa Cream, then the rice, 3 fish sticks, and a squeeze of the lime.

Roll up burrito style: bottom up, sides in, and then roll away from you.

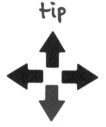

tip

Fish-Stick Shortcut
You want your fish sticks cooked and crispy, but you don't want them to take forever, so do this:

• Microwave however many you need for about a minute.

• Then cook them in a dry hot nonstick skillet on each side until lightly browned and crispy.

FROZEN POT STICKERS

Talk about your basic no-frills recipe. Buy them frozen in the market and follow the directions on the package. The trick is to microwave them and throw them into a hot pan to brown a bit. Then you serve them with the Sweet Chili Soy Sauce (page 44) or anything. Of all the Asian-y treats in the freezer section—these are one of the best.

FROZEN FRUIT

Remember what I said about frozen vegetables? That they're not just easier to deal with than fresh, they're just as good because they're picked when they're at maximum flavor, then sorted, separated, cleaned, portioned out, and quickly frozen? Well, the same thing applies here—and because they're frozen, there's no excuse not to have them around.

ZAMBA

This is often my son Zach's morning breakfast, his version of what you get at the smoothie shop. His brother Jordan thinks it's a "Zamba" because our last name starts with Z, but really it's because Zach created it. The Z is for Zach. Don't feel bad for Jordan: he has his own item in here too (just look up The Jo Jo on page 112).

Makes 2 smoothies

1 cup frozen mango chunks
1 cup frozen strawberries
1 banana, peeled and cut into
  large pieces
  Equal amounts of orange juice
  and cranberry juice—just
  enough to cover the fruit

Add the fruit to your blender and pour in the juices just to cover.

Start blending at medium speed so that everything begins to get chopped up.

Turn up the blender a couple of times and blend until everything becomes really smooth and well blended.

(NAME OF FRUIT HERE)
FROZEN MARGARITA

While I've never really been a frozen margarita fan, I do appreciate that many people are. And there's nothing better to use in them than frozen fruit. Peach, strawberry, mango—it doesn't matter. If it's in your freezer, the party is only 3 minutes away.

Makes 4 margaritas

1 cup frozen fruit chunks, plus extra for garnish
8 ounces tequila
½ cup ice
4 ounces sweet and sour mix
1 ounce Grand Marnier
½ lime

Put everything but the lime in the blender and blend until smooth.

Skewer a piece of the fruit you used and a little wedge of lime to put in each glass for garnish.

I've never really been a huge dessert guy, but I need to do something here, right? Actually, I just looked at some of these recipes, and they're pretty darn good. So maybe I'm becoming a dessert guy after all?

DESSERTS

- fresh mango & lime ice

- ten-minute mini cheesecakes

- peach & raspberry cobbler

- coconut macaroons

- the only 1-ingredient recipe I know

- world's best dessert waffle

- store-bought angel food cake

- frozen raspberry sauce

- very simple raspberry sauce

- chocolate & grand marnier fondue

- potato chip cookies

- mascarpone cream

- raspberry cream cheese won tons

FRESH MANGO & LIME ICE

The perfect dessert after a big-boy dinner. The recipe calls for rum and you can use whatever you like—but the coconut in Malibu® rum gives it an amazing tropicalness. Is that a word?

Serves 6

3 mangos, peeled and roughly chopped (save 4 mango wedges for garnish), or 3 cups frozen mango chunks
1 cup water
2 tablespoons sugar
Juice from 3 limes
¼ cup Malibu rum (trust me)

Add all ingredients to a blender and blend until smooth.

Pour into 9 x 13-inch baking pan and stick in the freezer until solid, 3 to 4 hours.

To serve, use a big spoon and scrape across the top to make a Hawaiian "shaved-ice" kinda thing. Serve in martini glasses if you have 'em, or something cool.

Garnish with the mango wedges.

TEN-MINUTE MINI CHEESECAKES

I use those little foil muffin cups that don't need a muffin pan for these. And okay, so you've gotta bake them for 25 minutes—but they still only take about 10 minutes of "hands-on" time. Make them for a party and let your guests top them the way they want.

Makes about 15

2 8-ounce packages cream cheese, softened
2 large eggs
½ cup sugar
1 tablespoon Grand Marnier
   Nilla® Wafers, about 15 (but get more because you'll eat them as you make this, trust me)

Preheat the oven to 325°F.

Combine the cream cheese, eggs, sugar, and Grand Marnier in a mixing bowl. Beat with an electric mixer or by hand until very smooth.

Drop one Nilla Wafer in the bottom of each muffin cup. Fill each cup ⅔ full.

Bake for 25 minutes, remove from the oven, and allow to cool completely.

Remove the foil cups and top with anything you like: fresh fruit . . . cherry pie filling . . . chocolate chips . . . jam . . . a pickle . . . whatever.

PEACH & RASPBERRY COBBLER

PEACH & RASP-BERRY COBBLER

This would rate about a zero out of ten on the difficulty scale.

Makes one 9x13-inch pan's worth—or serves about 12

2 16-ounce cans peaches in heavy syrup
1 10-ounce bag frozen raspberries
1 box yellow cake mix
1 stick butter, melted

Preheat the oven to 350°F.

Pour the peaches, syrup and all, into the bottom of a 9 × 13-inch pan.

Scatter the raspberries on top of the peaches.

Dump the cake mix over the peaches and pour the melted butter over the top, then spread the mixture around to cover the peaches.

Bake for approximately 40 minutes, until the cake is cooked and lightly browned in spots.

note

You ice cream people might enjoy a little vanilla with this. I'm not an ice cream person, but obviously that didn't stop me from mentioning it. That's because I care about you. I hate ice cream, but I care about you. What a guy . . .

COCONUT MACAROONS

Two ingredients—so easy . . . and soooo good. Mrs. Cooking Guy loves these.

Makes 12 to 15

6 ounces unsweetened coconut flakes

7 ounces (½ can) sweetened condensed milk

Preheat the oven to 350°F. Place a piece of parchment paper on a baking sheet.

In a bowl, mix together the coconut and condensed milk really well (this takes a little effort).

Form the mix into small mounds or pyramids.

Place on the baking sheet and bake for 15 minutes, or until golden brown.

Let cool (if you can wait) and eat.

THE ONLY 1-INGREDIENT RECIPE I KNOW

This makes a stupidly thick and rich kind of thing that tastes like an amazing caramel. The best way to eat it once cooled is on a spoon. You can try anything you want, but I'm telling you this . . . with a great cup of coffee . . . it's better than many things in life.

Makes 1 can's worth

I can sweetened condensed milk (BTW, this is not the same as evaporated milk)

Place the entire unopened can in the bottom of a deep pot. Cover the can with water at least 3 to 4 inches above the top of the can.

Bring the whole thing to a boil, turn down to a simmer, and let it cook for $2\frac{1}{2}$ hours. Now pay attention—it needs to stay covered with water the whole time.

When it is finished simmering, carefully remove the can and place in the fridge until cool.

Open the can, put some on a spoon, and the rest will just happen—trust me . . .

WORLD'S BEST DESSERT WAFFLE

When I was a kid, every night after dinner my dad Bruce would have vanilla ice cream topped with maple syrup and peanuts. He eventually developed some crazy stomach thing that got him cut off from the peanuts . . . bummer for him—but this is great for you. Make it. Oh, and apart from the waffles, all the amounts are approximate—but you'll figure it out.

Serves 2

2 frozen waffles
Vanilla ice cream (a good one—don't scrimp here)
Maple syrup or pancake syrup
Spanish peanuts (the kind with the red skins and salt on them)
Powdered sugar, for garnish

Toast your waffles according to the package directions.

Top with a scoop of vanilla ice cream, just not too much.

Drizzle with maple syrup and then top with a bunch of the peanuts.

Sprinkle with powdered sugar.

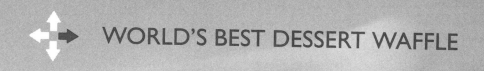

WORLD'S BEST DESSERT WAFFLE

STORE-BOUGHT ANGEL FOOD CAKE

I've always felt this is one of the more elegant desserts you can serve. And once again the cynics will judge me by this mostly nonrecipe—and once again I won't care.

Angel food cake, while not all that difficult to make, is certainly easier to buy. And once you have it, there is a ton do you can do with it. For instance:

- Serve it plain with a little whipping cream and a drizzle of chocolate, a liqueur, some fruit syrup, or almost anything

- Stick it under the broiler—that's right, bucko, put a little heat on it and the whole thing will change. Then it's just a matter of what you put on it, like ice cream, whipped cream, caramel, or even fresh fruit—or try this on top of the cake with ice cream:

FROZEN RASPBERRY SAUCE

Feel free to substitute strawberries or some other fruit. I just happen to really like raspberries as a sauce.

Makes about 4 cups

2　10-ounce packages frozen raspberries, thawed
¼　cup sugar
2　tablespoons lemon juice

Combine all the ingredients in a blender or food processor and buzz until smooth. Serve warm or cold.

OR HOW ABOUT AN EVEN EASIER VERSION?

VERY SIMPLE RASPBERRY SAUCE

I came across this by accident one day when I took some sorbet out of the freezer to warm up slightly before serving—and forgot about it. My mistake is for sure your gain . . .

Raspberry sorbet

Let it melt.

Pour it on something.

Trust me . . . a little melted raspberry sorbet drizzled on some vanilla ice cream sitting on top of a piece of toasted angel food cake is ridiculously good. Just don't forget, as I mentioned in the garnishing section, to add some powdered sugar or a little mint . . . something.

So if you can use melted sorbet as a topping for something, you can use any kind of melted anything as a topping—such as any kind of ice cream, right?

CHOCOLATE & GRAND MARNIER FONDUE

You . . . someone special . . .
the lights down low . . . candles
flickering . . . romantic music, and
a smooth dark chocolate fondue to
share . . . one fork . . . two mouths.
Or it could be just you and the
chocolate . . . whatever works, right?

3 ounces bittersweet chocolate
3 ounces milk chocolate chips
About ¼ cup whipping
   cream—a tad more might be
   necessary
1 tablespoon Grand Marnier

Put the chocolate, cream, and Grand Marnier in a small pot over very low heat. As the chocolate melts, stir it into the cream—you're going for a smooth, creamy consistency.

When it's there, put it in small bowls for your guests and serve it with your dipping stuff.

Now you need things to dip into it:

Pound or angel food cake, cut into cubes

Fresh strawberries, with stems for you romantics
Fresh orange or pineapple pieces

Marshmallow, nuts, or anything else you like chocolate on

POTATO CHIP COOKIES

I did a show with viewer recipes a while back and this was sent in by Lori (her grandmother used to make them). They are surprisingly good, and because of the sweet, salty, and crunchy combo, apparently also a big hit with women during their "special time," but I probably shouldn't get into that here.

Makes about 3 dozen

1 pound butter, softened
1½ cups sugar
2 teaspoons vanilla extract
3½ cups flour
5 ounces plain, thick-cut potato chips, crushed

Preheat the oven to 350°F.

Combine the butter and sugar in a mixing bowl.

Beat with an electric mixer until fluffy. Mix in the vanilla.

Add the flour until mixed well, then add the crushed chips and mix.

Drop teaspoon-size-ish spoonfuls onto a cookie sheet.

Bake until light golden brown on the edges, approximately 10 minutes.

Let them cool a bit before eating if you can.

MASCARPONE CREAM

These two little ingredients will glamorize absolutely anything you put them on or with—think whipped cream, but way better and richer. It can go on cake, pie, fresh fruit, beside some warm cookies as a decadent dip—almost anything.

Makes about a cup

4 ounces mascarpone cheese
⅓ cup whipping cream

Put mascarpone and cream in a mixer and blend until smooth. Refrigerate until ready to use.

RASPBERRY CREAM CHEESE WON TONS

The first time I made these, I pulled them out of the oven and asked Kelly (Mrs. Cooking Guy) if she wanted to try them. "Hot cream cheese—no, that's gross," she said and walked away. Why do I even bother, I wonder? So I take them up the street to Matt & Peg's, they not only try them, they LOVE them. So will you.

Makes 24

 8 ounces cream cheese
 2 tablespoons raspberry jam
24 round won ton wrappers
   Powdered sugar

Mix the cream cheese and jam well in a bowl, then put in the fridge for about 20 minutes—you don't want it too soft.

Meanwhile, preheat the oven to 400°F.

Put about 2 teaspoons of the cream cheese mixture in the center of each wrapper. Lightly moisten the edges of each wrapper with water. Fold in half, try to remove as much air as possible, and seal tightly.

Place the won tons on baking sheets. Bake until they start to brown, 15 to 20 minutes.

Remove from the oven and put on a serving plate. Dust lightly with powdered sugar and serve alone or with ice cream.

all done.